A DANGEROUS DELIGHT

Dangerous Delight

Women and Power in the Church

Furlong, Monica

SPCK   1991   14/8/2003

Source   LGCM Corporate Collection

What goes on between women and men, why men hold the power,
and why women so often collude with self-denigrating images and
expectations.

1355

Women's Issues, Feminism

MONICA FURLONG

A DANGEROUS
DELIGHT

Women and Power in the Church

First published in Great Britain 1991
SPCK
Holy Trinity Church
Marylebone Road
London NW1 4DU

Second impression 1992

British Library Cataloguing in Publication Data

Furlong, Monica, *1930–*
A dangerous delight.
I. Title
262.15

ISBN 0–281–04551–8

Phototypeset by Intype, London
Printed in Great Britain by
Dotesios Ltd, Trowbridge, Wilts

To Ronald Eyre

with whom I have had
the best conversations on
this subject

'I can't decide whether to be an actress or a bishop.'

Religion is power, it has to be, that power for instance to change oneself, even to destroy oneself. But that is also its bane. The exercise of power is a dangerous delight. The short path is the only path but it is very steep.

Iris Murdoch, *The Sea, the Sea* Chatto 1978, p. 455

Religion is potent. It is the most potent ideology the world has known for undermining the integrity of women as first-class members of humanity.

Daphne Hampson,
in debate with Rosemary Radford Ruether,
New Blackfriars, May 1986

Contents

Foreword

I am conscious that by devoting much space in this book to the struggles of women in the Church of England not only to become ordained but, more importantly, to change long-accepted prejudices and attitudes, I may appear to be ignoring the rather different experience of other churches who have already ordained women. I know, from writing on this subject in the past, that this can make the ideas seem irrelevant to Free Churches and Anglican churches abroad as well as suggesting that I have an annoying obsession with the storm in the Church of England teacup.

I have persisted, however, for several reasons. One is that I am far from sure, as a result of observation, that some of the churches who already ordain women ministers or priests are as far from prejudice and stereotyping of women as they would like to think. One of the merits of having all the skeletons fall out of the cupboard at once, as has happened in the Church of England in the last few years, is that the revelation of sexism becomes plain and undeniable, whereas in other places it is much less noticeable. Another reason I have stuck with the church I know best, apart from the fact that it *is* what I know best, is that I think that churches like the Church of England, the Roman Catholic Church and the Orthodox Churches, which place great emphasis on the sacraments, are those which show most clearly how deep the prejudices against women go. For though many anti-woman bigots can, with a gulp and an eye rolled heavenward, eventually digest the idea of women preaching, or caring for the flock, or praying or leading worship, their sticking point is revealingly identical – it is woman as priest representing Christ at the altar, or woman holding the holy objects of bread and wine. Woman as 'not quite Christlike' or woman as 'unclean' because of her menstruating and gestating functions is what most inspires fear, disgust or scorn, and it is the confrontation of that fear, disgust and scorn that interests me most.

My final reason is that I felt it a good idea not to generalize any more than I absolutely had to, but to be as specific as possible. It is *this* Church, *this* General Synod, *these* bishops, *these* clergy, *these* laity, *these* women and men, that I am writing about. I have to say, however, that I doubt whether some of the experiences described, the feelings acknowledged, the ideas discussed, will seem strange, unfamiliar, or irrelevant in any part of the world where such matters are of importance.

Monica Furlong
London
March 1991

Acknowledgements

I owe a particular debt to Sheila Fletcher's book *Maude Royden: A Life* (Blackwell 1989), Brian Heeney's *The Women's Movement in the Church of England: 1850–1930* (Clarendon Press 1988) and William Countryman's *Dirt, Greed and Sex* (SCM 1989), all of them invaluable works of scholarship in badly neglected areas.

The Movement for the Ordination of Women generously allowed me to consult their archives for material about women's ordination.

I am grateful to the following for permission to reproduce the cartoons: p. v, David Austin and *The Spectator*; p. 1, MOW's journal, *Chrysalis*; p. 13, Christian and *The New Statesman*; p. 69, *Chrysalis* (redrawn by Esdon Frost); p. 89, Richard Smith and *Chrysalis*; p. 129, Taffy Davies and *Chrysalis*. The cartoon on p. 51 first appeared in the Christian Conference of Asia Newsletter. The placard held by the priest read 'Struggle for Justice', pointing up the gender blindness of the liberation struggle in the third world. The British version is the work of Hazel Addy. I have not been able to trace the source of the other cartoons.

I am also grateful to Bridget Upton whose researches on my behalf were the greatest possible help.

1 · Silent in the Churches

*If I didn't happen to know that you have had no theological training
I would have said that your last remark was something
of very great importance.*

Let the woman learn in silence with all subjection. But I suffer not a woman to teach, nor to usurp authority over the man, but to be in silence. For Adam was first formed, then Eve. And Adam was not deceived, but the woman being deceived was in the transgression.

First Epistle to Timothy 11–14

Dominant groups describe subordinate groups as possessing those characteristics which are not part of their own self image – being emotional, passive, indecisive and weak. Dominant groups monopolize the functions to which most value is attached and prescribe other servicing roles to their inferiors. These roles are then justified by talk of 'natural differences'. Any questioning of, or protest about, these arrangements is seen as threatening anarchy. Objects are ignored, ridiculed or crushed according to the perceived extent of the threat.

And All that is Unseen: The Report of the Industrial and Economic Affairs Committee of the General Synod Board for Social Responsibility of the Church of England, 1986, p. 38

In the due subordination of woman to man for high and holy purposes the true dignity of woman consists . . .

Christopher Wordsworth, Bishop of Lincoln, 'Christian Womanhood and Christian Sovereignty'. A sermon, 1884

Some women leave [the Church] because it is too painful to stay; others stay because it is too painful to leave. Still others stay because they believe that the church, as the Body of Christ – neither male nor female, rich nor poor, 'coloured' nor white – has the possibility of renewing itself . . . they believe the church has the resources with which to create a new community of women, of men, and of women and men; it has the possibility of nurturing the transformation of familial and societal relationships.

Constance Parvey, *Christian Feminism: Visions of a New Humanity* (Harper & Row 1984), p. 175

Spent the evening at Flaubert's . . . we talked about Sade. 'He is the last word in Catholicism,' he said. 'Let me explain: he is the spirit of the Inquisition, the spirit of the medieval Church, the horror of Nature. There isn't a single tree in Sade, or a single animal.'

Pages from the Goncourt Journal, ed. Robert Baldick (Oxford University Press 1978), p. 14

THE QUOTATIONS opposite offer a sort of quick sketch of a change in Christian history, a change akin perhaps to the collapse of colonialism in the empires of this world, in which ideas, leaders and organizations undergo drastic alteration. Just as many native peoples eventually allowed themselves to notice their subjugation, to experience and utter their resentment, so Christian women, from about the middle of the nineteenth century, began to ask why they should be 'silent in the churches', why they should carry the stigma of Eve, why they should be deprived of all leadership in an organization to which many of them were deeply committed. Alongside of this they asked why others needed to subordinate them and what they gained by it, why they had themselves ceded vital power, and above all, how their subjugation was consonant with the beliefs the Churches claimed to hold. 'In Christ there is neither male nor female' the Epistle to the Galatians boldly claimed, yet the Churches drew gender boundaries wherever men and women looked.

As women found their voices and began to ask the troubling questions, the inevitable happened – they were accused of irrelevance, selfishness, stridency, unnaturalness. Ridicule, always a favourite weapon against women, was freely employed. Most telling of all, in an institution as ambivalent about power as the Christian churches, women were charged with having a lust for power. You might think power a natural thing to desire when you are permitted none, but within the context it was portrayed as a sign of women's worldliness and greed.

This book is unashamedly about power, the power to which women ask to be admitted in the Christian churches, and which men, and more particularly clergymen, refuse them.

It is therefore also about feminism, feminism among

women and men who hold Christian allegiance. Feminism throughout all the churches in the 1970s and 80s has gradually established an extensive critique of organized Christianity, of which the basic tenet is that it has been an instrument of oppression for women, in which attitudes about the Fall, God, authority, nature, sexuality and much else, have kept women in a subordinate and disadvantaged position. Since Christian thought and belief played such an important part in Europe and the New World in shaping Western society, so, feminists believe, to that degree it has unwittingly been the architect of a sexist society. Only as ecological arguments become more urgent do we also notice links between Christian attitudes to women with the emphasis on domination and control, and Christian attitudes to nature, attitudes which have damaged and impoverished the natural environment to the point where human survival, as well as the survival of innumerable species of creatures and plants, is itself threatened. 'What we do to the humblest of His creation,' wrote Thomas Merton in 1958, 'we do to Him.'

An added sharpness, a useful pointedness, has been given to the discussion by the debate about ordaining women to the priesthood. It is of much more importance that Christians change their attitude to women than that they ordain women as priests, yet this confrontation about why women cannot be ordained as priests made it possible at least to notice and talk about the sexism of the Church, as well as to observe whether fine words about women were carried over into deeds. The Church of England has, for about sixty years, but much more intensively in the last fifteen years, struggled with the issue of women's ordination. In the course of that struggle, conducted through innumerable speeches, meetings, articles and letters, every conceivable argument, for and against women's ordination, has been put forward. An inextricable part of the debate, unintentionally throwing new light upon the arguments, was much startling evidence about the way Christian men, particularly clergymen, regard women. Almost as revelatory were discoveries about the way women see themselves, about their lack of self-esteem and their subservience to authority. Attitudes hitherto implicit in the organization and attitude of the Church, and thus taken for granted and ignored by almost everyone, became explicit and, to many women at least, a source of astonishment.

If the Church (in all its forms, Orthodox, Catholic and Protestant) helped to mould Western thought and sexual attitudes, Western thought has, since the Enlightenment, begun to diverge considerably from Christian beliefs, bringing many angry charges about 'secularism' from the churches. Secular thought did not move particularly fast in its attitudes to women but in the late eighteenth and early nineteenth century questions were asked and ideas explored that gradually initiated extensive change. This new thought concerning women has been particularly deplored by some church leaders – by Pope John Paul II, for example, who, in his letter *Mulieris Dignitatem* (1988), explains that the home or the convent is the proper place for women, or Bishop Graham Leonard, who believes that secular ideas about feminism contaminate long settled views of women and their role that are essential to a sense of Christian order.

Certainly, in the secular sphere, women have begun to enjoy very different status, as evidenced by the fact that in British society, within a period of less than a hundred years, women have been admitted to university education and allowed to take degrees, have had the fields of education, medicine, law, accountancy, the stock exchange, banking and many other professions opened to them, have begun to enjoy equal suffrage rights with men, have (in the person of Margaret Thatcher) occupied the pinnacle of political power, have availed themselves of effective contraception and legal abortion, and have experienced a new and relatively fair system of divorce. At the turn of the century none of these things were true, and much legislation had still to be enacted to give women the most obvious rights – not merely the right to vote, but equal rights in the occupation of the marital home (The Matrimonial Homes Act, 1967), and equal rights and claims over children of a marriage (The Guardianship of Infants Act, 1925). Not until the late Victorian period did married women have rights over their own property, savings and earnings (Married Women's Property Acts, 1870, 1882) or the right to sue for maintenance in the case of desertion unless they were already stranded in the workhouse (The Married Women (Maintenance in Case of Desertion Act, 1886).

As we look back through the window of the past to that very recent period when women had no access to learning, professional jobs, money and property, a particular view emerges with startling clarity. It is the assumption that women were owned by their father or husband or brother. Like property they were at the disposal of their owners and were their financial and personal responsibility. Many fathers and husbands *did* take admirable care of daughters, wives and other female relations, yet if they did not do so, or treated them brutally, women were largely helpless to help themselves. Their position of being 'privileged property', like a beloved slave, deprived them of economic resource and personal confidence, which might have enabled them to break out of their confinement, and to survive if they did so. The change in women's situation, transformed by work, education, money, birth control, is so huge, so far-reaching, so fundamental in the way that it affects every attitude, that it is paradoxically hard to notice it or take it in. It is only as Christian leaders repeat the old slogans about women that the 'quiet revolution' in our midst stands out in stark, incongruous relief.

Women themselves object that the handicaps and injustices suffered by them are by no means all removed, that for working-class women many of the old problems remain, and that even for women in occupations where the obstacles appear to have been cleared – as, for instance, in the medical profession or in Parliament – conditions and prejudices are still considerable handicaps. Yet the growing public recognition of the unrealized potential of women, and the continuing vigour of the debate about women's oppression in which many able women can take part, suggest that the movement for change is still gathering strength and exploring creative possibilities. It may be that simple access to education and work opportunities, with all the valuable implications this has for women, by no means exhausts the process of self-discovery that women are undergoing. They may not wish to use these resources in precisely the same way that men do. Like all oppressed groups women have been kept from many processes of self-discovery and are still catching up on important lessons in uncovering their identity. Although endlessly mocked for 'apeing men' in their struggle for emancipation, their deepest wish has not been to 'be like men' but to discover how to be their own selves.

That process has gathered momentum and is already far advanced. Partly as a result of some of the above changes, partly because of some more mysterious current in human awareness, women's sense of a separate identity has begun to grow, and their sense of self-esteem, still in many cases very low, has begun to rise. With that rise, and the growth in feminist analysis, has come a shift in consciousness. Women have developed a new sense of existing in and for themselves in the same way that men do, not primarily, as in the past, as someone's daughter, wife or mother, not first and foremost as a 'helpmeet', even though some may be glad to be helpmeets to a beloved other person, but as persons in their own right. From this emerges a new strength, with a subsequent insistence on a different recognition – a demand, for example, of work being valued, of opportunity for education and fulfilling work being at least as available as it is for men, of a realistic control of childbearing potential, of the same sort of freedom from fear of sexual harassment, domestic violence or casual rape that most men enjoy.

It is this alteration of women's consciousness, one which many men have noted and (not without apprehension in some cases) understood, that the churches have tried to ignore, vainly trying to pretend that everything is still the same (or should be), and that with a little firmness they should be able to remain *in statu quo ante*. Upon this, some of them believe, the survival of the Christian faith depends.

A puzzling and confusing aspect of Christian attitudes to women is a particular sort of idealization of Woman in the person of the Virgin Mary, an iconization which, it has often been suggested, should rub off in a subtle kind of flattery of the female sex, particularly of those who conform most closely to the popular image of the Virgin – that is, as humble, passive, chaste and submissive. In exchange for their wish for some sort of control of their own lives and a sense of active participation in the world, women have sometimes been offered a sort of quasi-divinity, a place on a male-constructed pedestal on which they had only to keep still in order to be adored. It has been enormously tempting for women, particularly in societies which have offered them few genuine alternatives, to try to conform to the lineaments of the icon. Yet the small esteem or downright scorn for women who would not, or could not, conform to the idealization – childless women, strong, confident, sexual, intelligent, active women, or women who cared little for male approval – might have suggested how little the iconization of Mary as the eternal feminine benefited women in general, that in fact she was manipulated into being an instrument of oppression for women. What is sad is that this has come close to perverting one of the most important (that is, potentially healing) symbols of Christianity – the symbol of the baby held lovingly in its mother's arms.

It becomes obvious that one of the deep questions thrown up by Christian feminism is what sort of Christian faith we want to encourage. It seems likely that many people are drawn to the churches because of a dislike of change, and from a need to find at least one refuge where everything remains the same. Even a superficial reading of the gospels suggests that this is almost the direct antithesis of the intention of Jesus who seemed to have some more dangerous and exciting life-course in mind, but it would be foolish not to notice how prevalent this sort of conservatism is among churchgoers. More and more women, however, whatever their devotion to the profound symbolism and insights of Christianity, feel a decreasing attraction to institutions which assign them a subordinate status, which deny them not only leadership but, often enough, any voice in matters about which they may know more than 'fathers' in God – polygamy, female circumcision, birth control, fertility. Many women nowadays are able theologians as well as having a great deal of expertise in many matters that church fathers feel are their own province. Yet their opinions, however well-informed, are rarely sought after. They are treated like interlopers in a male club – that is, with a marked lack of benevolence, if not with downright hostility. Women, often very able, who would be welcomed in other professions, on offering themselves and their sense of vocation to the churches, are coldly dismissed, often with charges of delusion, or of having offered what Graham Leonard, speaking of women's ordination, described as 'an unwelcome gift' – he compared it, incredibly, to the Trojan horse of the *Iliad*. This extraordinary spectacle depicts the kind of dilemma that the Church of England poses for women.

Not all churches have such a poor record, of course. Within the worldwide Anglican Communion (to which the Church of England belongs) there are a number of provinces which have moved ahead and ordained women. In 1944 the Anglican Bishop R. O. Hall ordained a Chinese woman, Li Tim Oi, in Hong Kong, as a result of wartime exigencies (he was forced to withdraw her licence after the Lambeth Conference of 1948, though it was restored in the 1970s). In 1971 two other women, one of them an Englishwoman, Joyce Bennett, were ordained priest in Hong Kong, and in 1974 eleven women were 'irregularly' ordained in ECUSA, the Episcopal Church of America, in Philadelphia, USA. Two years later, in 1976, when ECUSA opened the priesthood to women, they and others were officially ordained. Canada, New Zealand, and other provinces – Kenya, Uganda, Brazil, Ireland – followed suit. In 1989 Barbara Harris was consecrated Suffragan Bishop of Massachusetts, and in 1990 Penelope Jamieson was consecrated as a diocesan bishop in New Zealand.

Anglican churches were far behind other Christians in allowing leadership to women. The Quakers, not having any form of ordination, have always allowed equal status to women. In 1917 the Congregational Church (now part of the United Reformed Church) began to ordain women to the 'full ministry of Word and Sacraments', to be followed at once by the Baptist Union, and, in 1974, by the Methodist Church.

The Church of England, having passed a Measure to remove legislation that debarred women from the priesthood in 1975, and the Measure to ordain women as deacons in 1987, then proceeded at a snail's pace with the legislation to admit them to the priesthood, issuing episcopal statements along the way that were themselves a source of offence to women. If the current legislation is passed in the early 1990s, it will, by the nature of the clauses, operate in a way that is discriminatory to women.

In the Roman Catholic Church, although there appears to be a monolithic opposition to women's ordination, many Catholics, both priests and lay people, are enthusiastic both about a more active role for women in the Church and also about women's ordination. Three thousand American priests, monks and nuns signed a letter applauding the consecration of Barbara Harris as a bishop in the Episcopal Church, and many Catholics in this country work for change. Even the Eastern Orthodox Churches, by far the most conservative in their attitudes to women, are beginning to reveal more complexity in their attitudes than had been expected, with certain key figures – Archbishop Anthony Bloom, Metropolitan of Sourozh, for one – showing sympathy with the idea of women's ordination.

In the Church of England opposition to change in the role of women within the churches comes from two main sources. On the one hand there are those, both women and men, who feel bitter distaste for change, in particular for the change involved in ordaining women to the priesthood, and are prepared to mount huge and expensive campaigns to block this development in any way they can. On the other hand there are those, mostly men, who claim a willingness for change but reveal by their endless qualifications, slowness, refusal to speak out where their views may be unpopular, and even more perhaps by a curious undercurrent of hostility in many of their utterances, their profound ambivalence. It is here, perhaps, that the unacknowledged sexism of our society can be most easily recognized, the sexism of

those who wish to regard themselves as tolerant and fairmin-
ded, but who actually dread the active participation of
women in the church, since it forces new kinds of growth.
In *Composing a Life* the American anthropologist Mary
Catherine Bateson quotes a black American woman as struggling simultaneously with racism and sexism. Of the two she
says racism is the easier to combat – 'You've got to get out
of the household at least for a moment to meet up with the
race question, but you wake up every morning meeting the
gender question, so you don't even notice it. It's pretty
intimate.' The universality and privacy of gender discrimination is part of what makes it invisible. 'You can zap racism
a lot easier because you have it expressed in the public
square.' And racists, she comments, do not as a rule share
their homes with people of other races. 'You're not gonna
have none o' *them* people in there with you, but you got
women in that household with you.'[1] Listening to clerics
in this country making impeccable liberal comments about
racism, it is difficult not to reflect that it is easy for them to
talk – race does not make any personal impact upon their
lives. If they change their attitudes to women, by contrast,
it has immediate personal impact, affecting their relationships to mothers, wives, daughters and women friends.
Hence, perhaps, the strength of resistance.

Such realizations did not come quickly to those of us
urging the ordination of women in the Church of England.
Most of us began the campaign with fairly simple ideas
about what it was we were trying to do, and only gradually
perceived the enormity of it. Attempting modestly to catch
a small fish – that is, to get women ordained – we were
astounded to discover that we had got Leviathan at the end
of the line, that unwittingly we had reached into the very
depths of the malaise not merely of the Church but of society
itself. Leviathan was, and is, only dimly visible to us – we
are still only partly conscious of what it is we struggle with
– yet it is unmistakably huge and important. It is connected
to the sick sexual fantasies of our society: fantasies of the
brutal use of power, humiliation of women, and rape, which
support a billion-pound pornography industry – fantasies

which lead to actual rapes and sexual assaults; and it is connected to male attitudes to women which make wife battering a commonplace. Is it possible that the adoration of women so evident in the cult of Mary is a form of denial of feelings of contempt and violence towards actual women?

Now I can imagine no way forward for the churches (and this may not be much less true for the churches that already ordain women than those rigorously opposed to it) that does not involve a further huge growth in consciousness for both men and women, the transformation in relations between men and women that Constance Parvey writes about in the quote at the head of the chapter. The Christian words for such a change are repentance and metanoia, the words of conversion. What is needed is a conversion in male attitudes to women, and in women's attitudes to themselves. With the mysterious synchronicity that we associate with movements of the unconscious this necessary conversion seems amazingly apt. For men to understand their ambivalence (that is, feelings of hate as well as love) towards women and to work with it creatively, may help us all to a different awareness of our ambivalence towards 'Mother Earth'. In both cases fear seems to have led to a need to impose a harsh will, and to a pleasure in sadistic exploitation, and in both cases the 'masters' – men over against women, human beings over against the rest of creation – chose an aggressive path that led to their own impoverishment, that allowed of no ultimate victory. There is time for change, not necessarily time to reverse all the damage that has been done in the past, certainly not time enough to prevent much of the havoc we have wreaked in the natural world, yet time to resolve fears, to cherish what we have abused, to conserve what we have squandered and plundered. This, I suggest, is the immediate Christian task.

Notes

1. Bateson, Mary Catherine, *Composing a Life* (Atlantic Monthly Press 1989), pp. 44, 46.

2 · Christian Stereotypes of Women: A Portrait Gallery

From *The New Statesman*

'My views are that women play a very important part in the church. They do the flowers, the cleaning. They show Christian virtues, no reason why they shouldn't be excellent women priests. No, I have no objections at all.'

Geoffrey Dickens MP, quoted in *The Correspondent magazine*, 25 February 1990

Swaddled in blue, the baby came home with mother. Keith personally helped them from the ambulance. As Kath started on the dishes, Keith sat by the fire and frowned at the new arrival. There was something wrong with the baby, something seriously wrong. The trouble with the baby was that it was a girl.

Martin Amis, *London Fields* (Jonathan Cape 1989), p. 6.

When some male students in the mixed college I was teaching at on the South Pacific Island of Papua New Guinea were asked to sleep on mattresses that might have been used by women, they vehemently refused. Gentle persuasion and rational argument made no impact on their resistance, but a head-on clash was averted by the idea of covering the offensive mattresses with plastic sheeting. Once the plastic was shown to be very tough and entirely waterproof tempers subsided and sleep became possible.

Alyson Peberdy, in Monica Furlong, ed., *Mirror to the Church* (SPCK 1988), p. 17

'Lo he abhors not the Virgin's womb'

'O Come All Ye Faithful'

Sir,
I wonder if it is possible to introduce a little commonsense into the argument by reminding ourselves of a few elemental and obvious facts?
A man is not a woman, nor a woman a man. Each sex is utterly different in spirit, mind and body. Each has his or her particular sphere of work.
In latter days a few women have penetrated into jobs pioneered by men, such as in schools, colleges, science, raiment, but they still gaze pathetically towards the male when the car won't go. A few women today seek the priesthood also. A few, I say, because the idea is obnoxious to the great majority of them.

Letter to the *Church Times* from Canon John Chapman, 14 February 1972

On the showing of both life and literature, women are nagging, treacherous, interfering, jealous and possessive: they deploy sexual charm and refuse sexual co-operation as and when best suits their intrigues of domination and venality. The female is sly, pestering, posturing, noisome and nosy.

Simon Raven in *The Sunday Correspondent*, 18 February 1990

THERE USED TO be a rather comforting idea in the churches – and you still hear it in some quarters – that the Christian Church had been a sort of model in its relations to women. Unlike some other religions which permitted polygamy, burned women on funeral pyres, or confined them in purdah, the Christians, following the example of Jesus, had always treated women with the utmost respect. One evidence of this was supposed to be the extraordinary devotion accorded to the Virgin Mary, and another was the veneration accorded to a handful of colourful women saints.

It is difficult for those brought up within such a belief (accompanied by the implication that gratitude is in order) to begin to question it, just as it is difficult for children to admit to unhappiness in a home where they are repeatedly told they are lucky. It is only as strength and confidence grow that it is possible to admit to unease, and to evidence that suggests that Christianity has not treated women well.

Slowly, timidly at first, tentatively, for at least a hundred years, women have been suggesting this. The pioneer American Elizabeth Cady Stanton, perceiving how many of the restrictions upon women, from ownership of her own property, legal custody of her own children, the right to an education, or even the chance to ride a bicycle, were given support by appeals to the Bible, produced *The Woman's Bible* in 1895, a formidable piece of biblical scholarship that challenged the suffering caused to women by the Christian *status quo*:

> The chief obstacle in the way of women's elevation today is the degrading position assigned to her in the religion of all countries – an afterthought in Creation, the origin of Sin, cursed by God, marriage for her a condition of servitude, maternity a degradation, unfit to minister at the altar and in some churches

even to sing in the choir. Such is her position in the Bible and religion.[1]

Maude Royden, Dorothy Sayers and many others in this country were to raise similar questions. What heightened the drama to the point where the basic conflict could no longer be ignored, however, was women's request for priestly ordination. Those churches who think in terms of ministers rather than priests eventually, though not very graciously, admitted women to their ministry. It was the churches with a sacramental emphasis – the Roman Catholic Church and the Church of England – who could not, and would not, move. Very, very slowly, the Church of England shifted, with a show of emotion that was a revelation. The insults, the temper, the hysteria, the insistence that 'there are far more important issues', and 'the time is not ripe', the banding together of extremist theological opponents, united only in this cause, the foot-dragging of the 'liberals', showed with pitiless clarity the determination to continue to deny women this form of leadership. If the ordination debate achieved nothing else, it would have been worthwhile simply to reveal the depth of bitterness and dislike towards women shown by many clergy. It lifted women out of a fools' paradise in which a general clerical benevolence towards them was assumed, to a place where they became acutely aware of the way stereotyping operates to keep power out of the reach of those thus abused. Only by dismantling the stereotypes, (often strangely contradictory, so that woman is both the universal temptress but also 'the angel in the house' and the sexless mother) can the Church gain any credibility in its talk of justice and love, in particular of the love between men and women. Women have to learn the trick of all those emerging from oppression – of refusing to be forced into the stereotype by social pressures. They have to achieve the more difficult task of becoming who they truly are.

Eve

The most fundamental of Christian stereotypes is the stereotype of Eve – woman as incurably treacherous. The quotation from Simon Raven given above plays on this primitive belief.

If you read the Bible literally, as most people did until recent times, then the story of Eve tells you what the original scandal was. Eve, the creature made out of a rib from Adam's side, listened to the serpent and did what God had commanded the human couple not to do – to eat of the apple from the tree of the knowledge of good and evil. She not only ate of the apple herself but gave it to Adam who promptly ate of it too. When accused by God of having broken the commandment he had given them, Eve blamed the serpent, and Adam, refusing to take any responsibility for his own action, blamed Eve. 'The woman . . . gave me of the tree, and I did eat.' The result was that both of them were turned out of Eden, Adam to toil for his food instead of living a life of bliss, Eve to endure the pangs of childbearing.

If we interpret this magnificent story mythically rather than literally, it claims that the ills of humankind derive from women's power to tempt, that this is the downfall of men who, were it not for women, would live in bliss. The Greeks have a similar story about Pandora in which it is a woman who, again as a result of curiosity, lets mischief forth into the world. In the first story, and probably in the second, there is a strong implication that we are talking about sexuality and the actions which remove us from the 'innocence' of Eden or childhood into a state of sophistication – 'the knowledge of good and evil', a dualistic state in exchange for a blissful unity.

Both stories are beautiful and haunting, both have extraordinary power, but both seem to look at the human predicament entirely from a male point of view. Countless women since the world began would claim that the events happen the other way round – that male sexual curiosity, and male seductiveness, have led them to eat of the tree of knowledge, and that this has led them in short order to the childbearing prescribed for Eve. In fact, one of the curious things about the Adam and Eve story is the sense of inversion of life as we know it. The man, oddly, gives birth to the woman by way of his rib, as if the author of the story cannot allow women their primacy as co-creators with God.

Whatever the intentions, conscious and unconscious, of the author of the Adam and Eve story, it came, very early in Christian history, to be used as it had been in Jewish history, as a pretext for blaming women and insisting that if they were not disciplined and subordinated to male power, then men would be endangered. (This lunatic logic has a disturbing parallel in the way that Christians, for centuries, persecuted Jews for having 'crucified Christ', knowing perfectly well that *these* particular Jews in medieval Europe were totally innocent of the crime, yet having such a strong need to work off feelings of anger that a 'representative' victim had to be found. Nowadays we know very well the appalling consequences of that kind of projection.)

It would seem to us now that women, down the centuries, have paid the price not just for the mythical apple, but for what it represents – the discovery of sexuality. It might have seemed a valuable discovery – akin to, or maybe a different expression of, Prometheus' discovery of fire – if Christianity, possibly influenced by the orgiastic cults of the Mediterranean in the first century and the need to be distinguished from them, or possibly swayed by the homosexual bias of Greek philosophy, had not developed such a strong distaste for 'the flesh' and such a strong conviction that it was inevitably in conflict with 'the spirit'.

Since, for the majority of men, attractive women were synonymous with 'the flesh', woman in the guise of Eve the temptress became the dangerous opponent of the new spirituality. She could not be eliminated entirely, of course – women were essential as bearers of heirs, as bringers up of children, as labourers within the home, even, as St Paul so chillingly says, as a prophylactic against lust, it being 'better' (less bothersome) 'to marry than to burn'. But so dangerous is woman thought to be that she needs male control, and the author of the First Epistle to Timothy describes how this is to be applied, and reminds his readers of the reason.

Let the woman learn in silence with all subjection.
But I suffer not a woman to teach, nor to usurp authority over
the man, but to be in silence.
For Adam was first formed, then Eve.
And Adam was not deceived, but the woman being deceived
was in the transgression. (1 Timothy, 2.11–14)

He also has instructions about how women should be
dressed: 'in modest apparel, with shamefacedness and
sobriety; not with broided hair, or gold, or pearls, or costly
array', and instructions about how the (male) deacon should
'rule' his household and his children. There is no advice
about how men should dress.

The injustice of the Epistle is palpable. Not only *was* the
man quite plainly 'deceived', not only did Adam seek to put
the blame, unfairly, on Eve, but if what he thought she
suggested was wrong then he behaved with a pathetic weakness that goes unmentioned. Yet Eve carries the blame for
him, and he escapes, at least to some extent, with his childish
irresponsibility.

Damaging as was the Jewish myth of Eve, the Christian
era, to begin with, undoubtedly made some differences in
attitudes to women. Jesus, after all, was born of a woman
who, according to the gospels, was specially chosen by God
for this privilege, and Jesus clearly cared deeply for particular women – Mary Magdalen, the sisters at Bethany, Mary
Cleopas, Salome – and spent time explaining his ideas to
women and healing them. Women remained at the cross
when the male disciples had fled, and were the first to witness
the resurrection. The New Testament mentions a number
of women as offering hospitality to the young church in their
own homes, and there seems little doubt that they were
among the early teachers of the Christian faith, and, later,
among the early martyrs.

Yet the new dispensation soon faltered. The Epistle to
Timothy, probably written early in the second century by
an unknown author, is already repeating the old canard
about women. Women should hold their tongues because
once, back in the golden age, they were the ones who spoiled
everything. Now they can never be trusted again, but must

remain firmly under men's domination. Not one word uttered by Jesus ever suggested any such thing, but his followers fell back comfortably into the prejudices of the ancient world, so convenient for male pride and selfishness.

Quite soon the Fathers were taking the story of Eve as accepted fact, and building an edifice upon it that was profoundly damaging to women. Clement of Alexandria (*c.* 150-*c.* 215) thought that 'the very awareness of her own nature must arouse a sense of shame in woman'.[2] Nearly every other Father joined the chorus of condemnation.

Picked up and embroidered by the Church Fathers, the idea that there was something *wrong* about women that demanded not only control, but punishment and contempt, spread and grew, with devastating effect. Tertullian and Jerome, Augustine and others echo the Adam and Eve story, women being seen as temptation incarnate, 'the gateway of the devil', 'a painted ill', the horrifying embodiment of the flesh, or nature, that against which intellect and spirit had to strive. As early as Origen, *c.* 185, as Peter Brown describes in *The Body and Society*, one sign of commitment among young Christian men was castration, the surgical removal of that which made men vulnerable to dangerous women and actually connected them to them in love-making.[3] Scapegoats of male lust, women were driven out, psychologically if not physically, into a wilderness bearing the sins, or at least the desires, of men.

The more that women were victimized the more it became necessary to justify the fact, since the story of Adam and Eve became a little thin as a reason for systematic relegation of human beings who revealed many engaging characteristics. The suggestion that there was something fundamentally 'wrong' with women – not simply that Eve had behaved badly, but that there was some structural or organic or severe character fault – completed the circular argument, showing that men were right to treat women as badly as they did. Much later St Thomas Aquinas (*c.* 1225–74) took his ideas about women from Aristotle, who described woman as 'a male *manqué*'. Aquinas may, in any case, have had little to do with actual women since he was taken from his mother and placed in a Benedictine monastery at the age of five, but was quite sure women were biologically monstrous. 'The particular nature of the active male seed intends to produce a perfect likeness of itself, and when females are conceived this is due to weak seed, or unsuitable material, or external influences like the dampness of the south wind.'[4]

But centuries before Aquinas spelled out the supposed biological inferiority of women St Jerome (*c.* 342–*c.* 420) was castigating women for their sexual appeal in letter after letter. Only a woman who was 'squalid with dirt, almost blind with weeping' fulfilled his criterion of a Christian woman. 'All night long she would beg the Lord for mercy, and often the sun found her still praying . . . continence was her luxury, her life a fast. No other could give me pleasure, but one whom I never saw munching food.'[5] Paula and other Roman women tried to reach Jerome's anorexic standards. In a letter of Christian counsel Jerome writes to a young girl, urging her to shut herself away from the world:

> What will you do, a healthy young girl, plump, rosy, all afire amid the fleshpots, amid the wines and baths . . . As you walk along your shiny black shoes by their creaking give an invitation to young men. Your breasts are confined in strips of linen, and your chest is imprisoned by a tight girdle. Your hair comes down over your forehead or over your ears. Your shawl sometimes drops, so as to leave your white shoulders bare, and then, as though unwilling to be seen, it hastily hides what it unintentionally revealed. And when in public it hides the face in a pretence of modesty, with a harlot's skill it shows only those features which give men when shown more pleasure.[6]

In the pathetic toils of repressed sexuality Jerome forgets he is writing to a devout young girl, and imagines her as a harlot.

Once again we have the sense of women, however personally good or innocent, being seen as representative, as a class, as the convenient source of blame for male disquiet. Indeed St Augustine went so far as to wonder why God had created them at all. The role of his unfortunate mistress, abandoned by him, though he took their child Adeodatus away with him at the time of his Christian conversion, has been made much of in his attitudes. Maybe the manipulative role of his mother, St Monica, so little concerned with his childhood sufferings when he was savagely beaten at school (according to the *Confessions*), so quick with her tears when his relationship with his mistress upset her in his adult life, has more to do with this than has been noted. Whatever the reason a bitter anger towards women seems to dictate his attitude, as it dictated that of most of the Christian Fathers.

It has taken women theologians – in the formal sense a very recent phenomenon – to show how comprehensive was the denigration of women and the rigour with which the Church attempted to discipline and control them. Uta Ranke-Heinemann notes, among much other repressive legislation, the Synod of Elvira (early fourth century) decreeing that women should neither write nor receive letters in their own name.[7]

Either because of suspicion of women, or because suspicion of women itself indicated some deeper dualistic malaise, many Fathers and Councils inveighed against sexual intercourse even within marriage, and seemed to feel that celibacy within a marriage would be a desirable norm. Significantly, ecclesiastical authority began to move decisively towards the idea of a celibate priesthood. Pope Leo IX (1002–54), following the reforms of Pope Gregory VII, enforced priestly celibacy, insisting that the wives of married priests were concubines. There were revolts, with some priests bravely marrying openly and others doing so secretly, but eventually the penalties for marriage became so severe that no priest of the Western Church dared to live with a woman except in secret. The wives of those already married often suffered terribly, being flogged, imprisoned and sent away without means of subsistence. Priestly celibacy was one of the key elements of the Gregorian Reform, and is thought to have played an important part in the Great Schism, the split between the Eastern and Western churches.[8]

Virtue seemed to be equated, not simply with abstaining from sexual intercourse, but with despising and rejecting women. St Bonaventure, in the middle of the thirteenth century, describes the saintly St Francis, the man who so deeply loved animals and was so kind to lepers, often regarded as the most Christlike of the saints:

> He bade that intimate intercourse with women, holding converse with them, and looking upon them – the which be unto many an occasion of falling – should be zealously shunned, declaring that by such things a weak spirit is broken, and a strong one ofttimes weakened. He said that one who held converse with women . . . could as little avoid contamination therefrom as he could, in the words of Scripture, go upon hot coals and his feet not be burned. He himself so turned away his eyes that they might not behold vanity after this sort that he knew the features of scarce any woman . . . he maintained that converse with women was a vain toy . . . [9]

(In contrast with ordinary women, or even with St Clare whom he treated in a cavalier manner that might be construed as cruelty, St Francis felt 'ardent devotion toward the Sovereign Lady . . . especial love for the Mother of Christ'.)

Aquinas's view of women as mutilated human beings became extended, rather like Hitler's racial theories about Jews, to prove that in every way woman was a disaster and a mistake, and that almost any mistreatment of her was justified. Perhaps it was only the sheer biological necessity of women, as childbearers, that prevented some sort of 'final solution' of the woman question, though the Middle Ages did witness a series of pogroms against women, under the guise of witch-hunting, some historians suggesting that they alternated with pogroms against the Jews.

It would be good to think that over the centuries the foolish habit of identifying all women with Eve had been dropped, that a greater love or discernment had developed towards women, either because of a growing psychological sophistication, or simply the straightforward evidence that relatively few women (when not driven by want) are prostitutes, that most are not obsessed with seduction or out to destroy men. Like men, women are people, trying to work and find good and comforting relationships to sustain them.

Yet the melodramatic vision of women as an unending source of temptation, plainly a titillating one to men, persisted. Because of it women were kept out of educational institutions, with important intellectual and economic implications for them, and where father or husband could afford it were kept at home, almost as a sign of conspicuous wealth. In 1884 two women's halls were set up in Oxford in the teeth of every kind of disapproval and opposition. 'What beguiled this University', thundered the Dean of Chichester from the chapel of New College,

> 'into taking the step which my friends and I did so greatly deplore . . . was, to speak plainly, the attractiveness of the inmates of the two Halls . . . The admirable ladies who preside over "Lady Margaret" and "Somerville" Halls and the charming specimens of young Womankind who made these Halls their temporary home – proved irresistible as an argument. The men succumbed. I remember once reading of something similar in an old Book. The man was very sorry for it afterwards. So was the woman.[10]

Worlds away from the author of Genesis, eighteen hundred years away from the birth of Christ, the story of Eve was still being used by clergy to deny women higher education. It continued to be used to enjoin silence upon them. As late as 1917, during the National Mission, a plan that permitted women to read out a call from the Bishop of London in church, was abandoned on these grounds. They were only to be permitted to speak to other women and children. Until the 1960s women were only very, very rarely permitted to preach.

The Harlot and the Witch

In the long centuries in which Eve has been condemned and punished there has been a hidden recognition of woman as powerful – so powerful that she can bring about man's downfall, so powerful that she must be rigidly controlled.

A figure of fascination in the Christian imagination has been the harlot who reforms – Mary Magdalen has been the model for this, although there is nothing in the Gospels to link Mary Magdalen to the woman who abased herself at the feet of Jesus and was said to 'have sinned much', and no evidence that that woman's sins were of a sexual nature.

Yet innumerable medieval artists lingered lovingly over the depiction of Mary the harlot, giving particular attention to her long red hair.

The Desert Fathers were to have many telling encounters with harlots, either ones whom they met processing triumphantly in the full splendour of the rich courtesan, ones who were penitent, or ones who, a little improbably, unless you take the view that they were the devil in disguise, arrived by night in the hermit's hut with the express intention of leading him into temptation.

Mary Magdalen and the harlots seem to have been welcome figures to prurient imaginations, much as news of Cynthia Payne is read avidly in the tabloids to this day. The harlots act out the male myth that all women are out to seduce; they are blamed and condemned for this seductive power. Some psychotics, like Peter Sutcliffe, the Yorkshire Ripper, feel that by murdering prostitutes they are righting a natural wrong, reproving a wickedness. Sutcliffe, like some of the Church Fathers, could not distinguish between prostitutes and ordinary women going about their normal lives.

The witch is a more ambiguous figure than the harlot. Sometimes she is seen as seductive, but much more often as the archetype any child can draw – the old woman with a pointed hat, a hideous face with an immense hooked nose and chin, a cat and a broomstick. (As a stereotype it is reminiscent of the caricatures *Der Stürmer* printed of Jews.)

The witch, in the traditional Christian view, is bent upon destructive magic. In league with the devil, she attends witches' Sabbaths and indulges in disgusting sexual practices. According to the *Malleus Maleficarum* (*The Hammer of Witches*) (1487), the famous treatise on witches compiled by the notorious Dominicans Jacob Sprenger and Heinrich Kramer, designed as a sort of handbook for the Inquisition, 'witches . . . collect male organs in great numbers, as many as twenty or thirty members together, and put them in a bird's nest, or shut them up in a box, where they move themselves like living members and eat oats and corn as has been seen by many and is a matter of common report.'[11]

Common report is often a dangerous witness – we can

imagine what, in our own day, *The Sun* would make of such prejudiced tattle. The force of Sprenger and Kramer's 'hammer' was that witches were a threat to male potency, though also to other forms of natural creativity – the growing of crops and the fertility of animals. How much, one wonders, did male guilt at the way women were abused and suppressed, cause men, and clergy in particular, to project such extraordinary images of violence upon women? The irony was that, while they were dying in their thousands (some say millions) in medieval Europe, implicating themselves and others under gross forms of torture, they were credited with extraordinary magical abilities. Upon this cruel myth was built a systematic persecution unrivalled until Hitler's holocaust.

Karen Armstrong quotes the witness of contemporaries of Sprenger and Kramer on the subject of witch torturing and trials:

> Some men who witnessed their terrible sufferings were appalled and spoke out against the persecutions. The Jesuit Friedrich von Spee went prematurely grey after his experience at the witch trials in Westphalia and Franconia. He was certain that innocent people were being executed: 'I confess that I would at once admit any crime and choose death rather than such suffering and I have heard many men, religious and of uncommon fortitude, say the same. What then is to be presumed of the female, fragile sex? I know that many die under enormous tortures, some are crippled for life, many are so torn that when they are beheaded the executioner does not dare to bare their shoulders and expose them to the people. Sometimes they have to be hurried to the place of execution lest they die by the way.'[11]

The two terrible biblical texts, 'There shall not be among you a witch' (Deuteronomy 18.10) and, 'Thou shalt not suffer a witch to live' (Exodus 22.18) were cited again and again to justify the extreme of cruelty.

Everything we know now suggests that many of the women destroyed in this way were old, eccentric, maybe expert in herbal medicine, but often completely innocent of any fault. What, we may wonder, made them seem such a threat as to merit wholesale destruction in such a cruel manner?

One of the theories about Hitler's persecution of the Jews was that they were a convenient lightning conductor whenever political dangers threatened. Each time there was a military or other setback, rage could be deflected from the real source on to an increasingly helpless and terrified group, who had no means of resisting. Perhaps attacks on women, fuelled by the repressed sexuality of a largely celibate society, were a distraction, a whipping up of a perverted religious fervour for political or theocratic ends (Ranke-Heinemann shows that the days of the year when married couples in medieval Europe were not permitted to have sexual intercourse added up to around five months, which did not include abstinence on account of menstruation or childbirth). (Even in our own time it seems possible that some of the charges of satanic abuse, few of them substantiated by facts, may be fulfilling a similar function.)

Yet I suspect some of the reasons go much deeper. The supposed witches, like the Jews, were reminders of a religion much older than Christianity, and were thus regarded as a source of potential subversion. The witches, with their herbal remedies and their interest in the rhythms of nature, hark back to earth religion, to a faith not of domination of nature but of harmony with it.

In modern language and thinking we would describe the witch as a 'shaman', someone with insights that go beyond the every day, who may know how to fly, to speak the language of animals, to heal, to teach rites important to the proper working of nature, to have dreams important to the survival of the group, but whose primary purpose is integrating humankind within the rhythms and disciplines of the natural world.

With the help of anthropologists it is possible to look at the work of shamans in primitive societies and to note the important and powerful role they played, having been carefully prepared by exacting ordeals and rituals to integrate the human animal within the rhythms of nature.

To take one example, the *karadji* of Australian aboriginal

culture, James Cowan writes of them like this: 'In any living tradition there must always be cultural exemplars who reflect a condition of primordiality which is a link between the natural and supernatural worlds. Such men (and occasionally women) possess certain qualities of behaviour and, more properly, a presence that others may recognize as distinctively different.' Cowan goes on to describe the particular spiritual disciplines that such people underwent, disciplines that taught them healing skills, largely by the process of being able to 'see' physical disease, perceive the root of mental disorders, exorcise demons – in other words develop extraordinary powers of discernment. What the *karadji* had is *miwi*, or power, something which everyone has to some degree but only a few develop. It is situated, they believe, in the pit of the stomach. Like the Hindu *kundalini* process, with which it has strong similarities, it is about spiritual vision and transformation.

> The *miwi*, when developed, can precipitate a restoration of the primordial state and so bring about man's recovery of his sense of eternity . . . (the *karadji*) was one of the few people able to create new dances, songs and stories. Through him a tribal community could remain culturally vital and grow accordingly . . . The importance of the *karadji* as resident tribal sage and seer cannot be overestimated. The arcane information at his disposal was a constant source of spiritual security among other tribal members who looked to him for answers in times of uncertainty.[13]

Amongst other accomplishments the *karadji* was thought to be able to fly.

When the white man came to Australia the *karadji* very quickly came under attack. He was, says Cowan, regarded as 'subversive' by the Christian missionaries and others

> precisely because he stood for a dimension of spiritual experience unattainable to those in question . . . Squatters had him driven from the land or executed; missionaries and teachers made every attempt to undermine his spiritual authority through the introduction of alien beliefs; doctors brought into ridicule his use of traditional remedies by the use of flagrant modern medicinal techniques; observers and, more latterly, anthropol-

ogists emphasized the sorcery aspects of his profession to the detriment of his spiritual attainments. In the end, Aboriginal traditional society was effectively destroyed when the *karadji* as cultural exemplar was considered to be redundant. His *miwi* power flowed from him and was eventually lost. The spiritual knowledge and the ascetic disciplines that needed to be practised for its attainment have now all but been eradicated. What was left were the remnants of a traditional society trying desperately to make sense of a world that only he had the power to under-stand.[14]

The *conjunctio* between the supernatural and natural worlds that the *karadji* represented, together with the rituals, meditation and insight that accompanied it, was lost along with the *miwi* power.

It would be inaccurate, of course, to see too close a parallel between the witches of our own history and the wise men and women of a very different culture, yet there are striking echoes of people able to use healing techniques and herbal remedies unknown to modern medicine, and with a closeness to nature that we have lost. There is something reminiscent too about the ferocity with which this ancient wisdom was hunted down and destroyed by a newer religion certain of its own rightness and blind to what was being lost.

The film *Yaaba* (Director: Idrissa Ouedraogo, 1990) from Burkina Faso in West Africa gave a fascinating opportunity to observe a slightly different interaction between witch and community in an African village. Yaaba is a very old woman, driven out of her native village as a child because both her parents died suddenly in an epidemic and she therefore represents 'bad luck'. She lives in a shack some distance from the village, denuded of everything, poor to the point of near starvation, and mocked. But in her lifelong exile Yaaba has developed uncanny intuitions and insight and gifts of healing, which she is prepared to use for the benefit of the community that rejects her. The men of the village, however, project enormous hostile power onto the kindly Yaaba, and when a little girl falls dangerously ill and is near to death, they burn down Yaaba's hut and drive her away.

Both Yaaba, and the women of the village (who believe

in her healing gifts) illustrate patterns in women's lives not at all uncommon in very different societies. Excluded from much that they might have enjoyed, they develop more covert forms of power, partly in self-protection, partly from feelings of despair and aggression. But this very ability to find power in powerlessness adds to mens' feelings that women are uncanny, and the projections upon them grow.

If there are such things as shaman-like powers and insights (and in a scientific world view it is hard for us to make this imaginative leap) then the evidence of many parts of the world is that they tend to be more for good than for evil, though the possibility of wicked powers is there if you believe in shamanic powers at all. Christian propaganda, insisting that all witches were wicked, was plainly biased and corrupt, and caused untold suffering. Perhaps already a new sense of the witch as healer is gaining ground, yet alongside that are growing terrors of satanism, and wild accusations of satanism and child abuse that must make us wonder whether the old persecutions could return.

A year or two ago, on holiday in Shetland, I read the report of an eighteenth-century Shetland woman who was nearly burned as a witch. When her fiancé was about to leave for a voyage she warned him of a premonition she had had that the voyage would be dangerous. When, later, news came that the ship had gone down, the young woman was tried as a witch and sentenced to burning. Only the fortunate arrival of the fiancé, who had survived the shipwreck, saved her from death by witch-hysteria.

Unclean

William Countryman in *Dirt, Greed and Sex* has written admirably of the effect the 'purity taboo' had upon the life of Jewish women in the pre-Christian era, and the way in which that taboo has been carried over into the Christian Church, although theoretically no such taboo exists in Christian theology.[15] In Judaism, blood, along with some other bodily fluids such as semen, equalled uncleanness. During an Orthodox Jewish woman's menstruation it was forbidden for her husband to lie with her, and after it she had to attend the *mikvah*, or ritual bath, to cleanse herself before intercourse could be resumed. While a woman bled – and some middle-aged women, like the 'woman with an issue of blood' whom Jesus healed in the gospel, bleed for months or years on end – no one might touch her bed, or sit on her chair, or sit with her at table, without also becoming unclean. Not only women were unclean – a man might become unclean by spilling his semen during a wet dream – but for the man, cleansing, and return to normal life, was quick (he needed to spend only a day away from the Temple) whereas for women the taboo was so powerful that it might exclude her from much of normal life for years at a time. It is painful to reflect just what this must have meant in terms of social exclusion for many middle-aged women.

The Jews were not unique in practising such a taboo – many peoples have felt a sort of mixture of wonder and horror at the sight of blood, recognizing that it was one of the great tokens of birth and death and life, yet the practical consequences of the taboo for women was one of exclusion from the life of the mind (regardless of whether or not they were gifted in that way) and, in part, of the spirit (the daily teaching and prayer in the Temple).

Many primitive peoples illustrate the kinds of terror that exist around women's creative powers, terrors that Christianity would treat contemptuously as superstitious if found in the mission field, yet which may continue to influence the treatment of women in our own society in hidden ways. In *Mirror to the Church* Alyson Peberdy, writing as a sociologist, describes a tribe, the Huli, in Papua New Guinea, where the women's menstrual and sexual fluids are regarded as dangerously 'polluting' for men. In the days around menstruation, pregnancy, or the years around the menopause, women are thought to give off a destructive 'heat'. 'The effects of this heat and of the woman's smell can cause a man's intestines to twist and tangle until they knot and the colon bursts . . . just one indiscretion can lead to a man's death.'[16]

The extreme danger experienced around women in practice restricts Huli women's lives extraordinarily. They must stay away from fishing, hunting, and male rituals, for fear of contaminating the food and destroying the prosperity of the tribe. In domestic life they are hedged around with innumerable restrictions. Rigidly controlled at home, they are also excluded from all power within the society.

No doubt compared with such a society women's role in the history of the Christian Church seems rich and satisfying. Yet the fact remains that, just like any Huli woman, within the Catholic and Orthodox traditions of Christianity, women have been excluded from nearly all ritual, from Councils and Synods, and from priesthood, and, until recently, from almost every sphere of social and cultural life except the domestic.

Does the 'contamination' of birth and menstruation play a part in this, a pale imitation of Jewish practice no doubt, yet more of a continuation of it than a break with it? It is often suggested that the 'Churching of Women', common in England until the 1930s, carried a sense of being 'cleansed' after childbirth, though its content spoke only of gratitude for a safe recovery from labour. More significantly, there are parts of the world where women are forbidden to receive Communion while menstruating, or, in some Eastern Orthodox countries, forbidden to touch a priest at that time. The hidden taboo expresses itself also in ancient superstitions – that women may not enter the vaults of wine-growers in France when menstruating, for fear of 'turning the wine sour'. Some famous French chefs forbid women in their kitchens from a belief that their menstruating presence might curdle the sauce.

All this seems a long way from the idea that Christians were 'different' in their attitudes to women, and from Jesus apparently not minding in the least when the 'woman with the issue of blood' touched the hem of his garment and was healed of her disabling condition – though she must have made him technically 'unclean' in the process.

What is bewildering, and frightening, to women in all this, is finding themselves somehow unacceptable not because of any moral misbehaviour or failure on their part, but simply because of their biological nature, as potentially givers of birth. We do not recognize ourselves in the stereotype of uncleanness until the stereotype has done its work upon our self-esteem.

Inferior and Helpmeet

Whether coincidentally or as a consequence of the Adam and Eve story, women in Judaic society occupied an inferior position. The devout Jew thanked God daily that he was not a woman. Wives, like children, concubines and slaves, were owned by the father-husband. They were not required to love him, though some doubtless did; their role was to bring him sexual satisfaction and profitable family connections, and in addition to play a vital part in household labour. Their most important function, however, was that they provided heirs. The relationship was one of total inequality – the man could divorce the woman, but not the woman the man. Adultery was a very different offence from the one we know. 'Adultery meant a man taking the womb and family resources which belonged to another man and using them for the nourishment of his own seed.'[17] Philo was to say that a man who raped a widow or divorced woman should not be punished because, after all, he had not offended against an interested male party.

The Judaic woman was, therefore, in some important senses a 'non-person', yet in practice, as reading the Bible makes clear, many women had a profound effect on the men whom they gave birth to or married, inspiring love, fear, and a variety of other emotions. The odd sense of women being officially totally unimportant, but privately, or secretly, very important indeed, is one of the baffling things, another of the open secrets, which confuses discussion on the subject to this day.

According to the Victorian Bishop Christopher Wordsworth, and many others, the taking of the rib from Adam's side to create Eve, had all kinds of implications about the future relations of men and women. In his sermon on Christian Womanhood in 1884 Wordsworth warned woman against imagining that she is independent being (*ousia*). Rather, she is *exousia*, that is, out of another being – (*exousia* also means 'authority'). Upon this fragile foundation, Wordsworth builds a huge edifice of seeming logic to prove to 'woman' that she is only truly herself when she is dependent and 'in subjection'. (An historical irony is that the Bishop's daughter, Elizabeth, was the first principal of Lady Margaret Hall, Oxford.) Such subjection, Wordsworth thinks,

> is the true source of (woman's) beauty and dignity. Not by usurping what does not belong to her, not by casting off the mark of her derivative being and subordinate authority, can she hope to retain the place which God has given her in creation . . . God has created woman from man and for man. Not to be a slave or a paramour, but to be a helpmate . . . anything which disturbs that subordination weakens her authority, and mars her dignity and beauty. Her true strength is in loyal submission; her true power is in love and dutiful obedience.[18]

The bishop's mixture of flattery and warning is both familiar and cunning. If for a woman to question her inferior position is to lose even the secondary claim to authority (i.e. dignity and beauty) that she has, then she is in a double-bind. Whether she speaks out, or is silent, she is caught. She cannot truly consent to an inferior role – no one can without profound damage to their self-esteem – she can only be browbeaten, forced into it, by some such device as Wordsworth employs.

Others came at the problem by making sure that women's self-esteem remained low. Many tyrants have noticed that education is dangerous to their authority in heightening the confidence and self-esteem of those they wish to exploit, and making them much more vocal.

Women's desperate struggle for education is too well known to need recounting here. John William Burgon, Dean of Chichester, deploring women's arrival at Oxford, worried (rightly, I dare say) that all this education would make women less amenable.

> Woman is intended to be Man's 'help' – Man's helper. The expression 'meet for him' implies that she is to be something corresponding to him – a second self yet not a rival self: for, as the Spirit pointed out some 4000 years later (i.e. after the Adam and Eve episode), man was not created for the woman, *but the*

woman for the man and from this very consideration the Spirit deduces woman's inferiority.[19]

Part of the function of woman as helpmeet, as Burgon goes on to say, is to be 'an influence' on men. In case they suppose that all power has been taken from them they should reflect on the fact that strong men, the strong men who run the great big world, are in reality totally controlled by them. 'We men are, to speak plainly, *just what you make us.* The weaker sex indeed you are; and the weaker sex you will forever be: yet, strange to relate, your very weakness is your strength. . . . Your reasoning is not always first-rate to be sure. . . .'

The world that women think they see, and experience, Burgon says, is deceptive. Largely deprived of education, of economic independence, of voting rights or protective legislation, repeatedly told that they are inferior, confined to the home and to a subordinate role, they may, with their poor weak minds, get the idea that they count for little. In fact, because of their gentle, unobtrusive influence upon men, they run the world. In some almost totally baffling way their weakness turns out to be strength.

But Burgon, thundering away about the dangers of higher education for women, knows that the work of demolition has started – that Somerville and Lady Margaret Hall threaten the comfortable world in which women are never rivals and are always at hand with the warm slippers and the encouragement. Women have stirred in the sleep of centuries and are beginning to wake up. The angel in the house is beginning to shake her wings.

Nineteenth-century clerics had a comfortable sense of women's inferior role, or rather, as Charles Gore ingeniously put it, woman's place involved 'a subordination which . . . involves no inferiority whatever in nature or essence, but only difference of function'.[20] The Reverend R. W. Harris addressing the 1902 Church Congress told women: 'Your real influence does not lie in public life and never will. It lies in the power you exert over men, individually and personally.'[21] 'Influence', says Brian Heeney, quoting this remark, 'was conceived as the real power of fundamentally subordinate and domestic women.'[22] Inevitably, unavoidably in the circumstances, women did use 'influence' to manipulate men into doing what they wanted, since this covert, dubious form of power was the only one permitted to them.

Despite being continually exhorted to the domestic role, nineteenth-century women played a huge role outside the home, doing much of the Church of England's work for it for nothing. Partly because many upper- and middle-class women from prosperous families had more time on their hands than ever before, partly because the needs and suffering of the poor were so acute, partly because of women's age-old instinct for devotion, huge numbers of women worked in slums and Sunday schools, as 'district visitors', in various kinds of 'rescue' work, and on behalf of overseas missions. In February 1917, Emily Wilding Davison mentioned the figure of 85,000 district visitors of whom 75,000 she said were women. Brian Heeney comments: 'Observers were aware of a vast volunteer enterprise, predominantly female in composition, clearly forming a major part of Victorian women's "church work" and persisting well into the twentieth century.'[23] In the first Church statistics of recognized reliability in 1883 there were some 100,000 women Sunday school teachers (out of some 113,412 teachers). This was also the era of the rise of the Girls' Friendly Society – a movement among wealthier or better educated women to help working-class girls – and of the founding of the Mothers' Union.

But neither their unremitting hard work, their enthusiasm, nor their devotion did much to change women's status. As late as 1926 there was argument in a paper called the *Church Militant* 'as to whether women should communicate before men, or after, to indicate their subordination . . . it was quite acceptable in Anglo-Catholic circles to argue the question of whether women should wear hats in church, or even to discuss the effects of menstruation.'[24]

One of the biggest humiliations of women in the Church of England concerned parochial church councils, and subsequently the Church Congress (which preceded Church

Assembly and General Synod). The early years of the twentieth century showed an impressive movement to give the laity a bigger part in the government and power of the Church, (because of the threat of dissenters and disestablishment) and it was this which brought parochial church councils into being. But though Christian lay*men* were offered a bigger part in the councils of the Church, laywomen were excluded. In May 1897 the bishops in the Upper House of the Canterbury Convocation adopted six resolutions designed 'to quicken the life and strengthen the work of the Church' by encouraging the formation of parochial church councils. The fourth of these stipulated that 'elected councillors be male communicants of the Church of England of full age'.

The bishops themselves disagreed about the exclusion of women, and this uncertainty, according to Brian Heeney, 'provoked the first clear expression of Church feminism'.[25] Eleven hundred churchwomen signed a petition and presented it to the Upper House in February, 1898, protesting against the ban on female candidates for parochial church councils. It was sixteen years before their protest achieved results.

The embryo of Christian feminism was encouraged to grow when, in July 1903, the Representative Church Council was formed. Not only could women not stand for this – they were not even permitted to vote for representatives. It took until 1914 for this battle to be won.

Theories about women's inferiority and subordination surfaced repeatedly during the women's ordination debate between 1975 and the time of writing (see Chapter 5). It was not always noticed how far and how fast the world around the Church of England was changing.

A Weak Creature

In 1981, the year after Margaret Thatcher had become Prime Minister, Dr Robert Runcie gave a speech at a World Council of Churches conference at Sheffield on The Community of Women and Men in the Church. He began with a recognition of the way ministry had been taken from women, or rather the way that women's very genuine ministries within the churches had lacked recognition. He went on, rather nervously, to consider 'the women's movement', over against 'feminism', which he saw in terms which made it appear ludicrous and unrecognizable to many who belong to it, but which implied fear. 'The women's movement today is no longer simply feminist . . . It divides between those who want to burn their bras, refuse to marry, and insist on doing all that men do – even to playing games which are anatomically painful – and those who ask for something more difficult to articulate.' That something was a freedom not to be constrained by male attitudes, but which (a puzzling emphasis) 'has often to accept a measure of physical weakness. This may breed not militancy but a very real humility.' He went on to suggest that women's complexity may be a source of fear to men.[26]

This well-meaning speech, with its travesty of feminism, and its insistence on female weakness and necessary meekness, though dressed up in more amiable terms than in nineteenth-century sermons, was heard as condescending; the tone of voice spoke more loudly than the words (and they were loud) in showing that the old beliefs and inequalities were alive and well.

There were not many more speeches about female frailty as the eighties wore on – perhaps because Mrs Thatcher's phenomenal strength cast a doubt upon all female fragility.

Dr Runcie stood in a long tradition, of course. From 1562 onwards various homilies on marriage were scheduled to be read every Sunday in Anglican churches. To quote one: 'The woman is a weak creature not endued with the strength and constancy of mind; therefore they be the sooner disquieted, and they be the more prone to all weak affections and dispositions of mind more than men be; and lighter they be and more vain in their fantasies and opinions.'[27] The historian Lawrence Stone quotes this as a part of a systematic subordination of women (and children) to the whims and needs of men, a subordination in which the Church was a leading advocate, and quotes Defoe on suggesting that wives were little more than slaves or, at best, 'upper servants'.

It was striking how often comments about women's physical weakness quickly passed into the suggestion that they were mentally unstable, as above. The effect on women of being continually told that they are silly, frail and stupid, especially when coupled with an inadequate education that made it difficult to hold their own in reasoned argument, was that, inevitably, they took the denigration for truth and rapidly internalized it. Even supposedly dispassionate observers, such as Freud and Jung, contributed their own biased viewpoints, Freud by treating male experience as if it was the norm for all human beings and women as if they were physically mutilated (a bit like Thomas Aquinas' idea), and therefore understanding women almost entirely in terms of their supposed envy of the male member, and Jung (who also noted women's envy) by declaring that women who were vociferous in complaining of their lot were under the pathological domination of what he called 'the animus'. Like Bishop Wordsworth they had hit upon devices which made it hard for women to protest: Bishop Wordsworth found women who protested immodest and unattractive. Freud and Jung thought them sick.

The irony of so much talk of women's frailty is that it only seemed to be mentioned when it was a useful way of excluding them from opportunities – work, education, etc., that they desired. In fact, throughout history, women's extraordinary strength, courage and stamina has been repeatedly observed. 'Ain't I a woman?' asked the American slave Sojourner Truth, when she heard that women were too weak to minister. She recalled her own life of unremitting physical toil in the fields, herself burdened, as her male companions had not been, by gestating and childbearing. More than half a century before, Charles Lamb, writing with splendid scorn of claims in his day to protect women and treat them with deferential respect, said that

> I shall believe that this principle actuates our conduct, when I can forget, that in the nineteenth century of the era from which we date our civility, we are but just beginning to leave off the very frequent practice of whipping females in public . . . I shall begin to believe that there is some such principle influencing our conduct, when more than one-half of the drudgery and

coarse servitude of the world shall cease to be performed by women.[28]

Maude Royden, writing during the First World War of her experiences in a maternity hospital, where she watched working-class women giving birth without any anaesthetics to ameliorate their pain, said 'There they will see, to match the heroism and the sacrifice of the soldier, an equal heroism, an equal sacrifice, but without Victoria crosses. . . . There they will see the war which women suffer to bring life into the world.'[29]

When it was convenient women were frail. When it suited society for them to be strong, as in two World Wars, then no burden was too great for them to bear.

Virtuous

One of the puzzles about stereotypes of women is that woman is simultaneously told she is treacherous and seductive, but also is of irreproachable virtue. Sometimes this occurs in the same passage or poem as in

> O Woman! in our hours of ease,
> Uncertain, coy and hard to please . . .
> When pain and anguish wring the brow,
> A ministering angel thou![30]

She was supposed to be a little 'daffy', like David Copperfield's Dora, so that men could advise and correct her, yet severely practical and helpful when men needed her services. In the nineteenth century, in addition to being a little silly, a 'lady' was required to be sexually coy and inhibited, brought up, like Lady Bracknell's Gwendolen, 'to know nothing'. Sexual pleasure was not to be admitted, and it may well have been rare. A lady did not move.

The idea of women as entirely asexual was part of another way of removing women from an active role in the world, that of idealization. A bizarre view of women emerged in the Archbishops' Commission in 1936 to explain – the first of many such statements to come – why it was impossible for women to be priests. It was quoted with amusement by Virginia Woolf in her book of feminist essays, *Three Guineas*:

We maintain that the ministration of women will tend to produce a lowering of the spiritual tone of Christian worship, such as is not produced by the ministrations of men before congregations largely or exclusively female. It is a tribute to the quality of Christian womanhood that it is possible to make this statement; but it would appear to be a simple matter of fact that in the thoughts and desires of that sex the natural is more easily made subordinate to the supernatural, the carnal to the spiritual, than is the case with men; and that the ministrations of a male priesthood do not normally arouse that side of female nature which should be quiescent during the times of adoration of almighty God. We believe, on the other hand, that it would be impossible for the male members of the average Anglican congregation to be present at a service at which a woman ministered without becoming unduly conscious of her sex.[31]

This statement, clearly honed in the Wits' End Department of the Church of England, calmly reverses generations of gibes about Eve and Mary Magdalen. *Now* woman's problem is that she is *too good* to be a priest.

Mother, Madonna

> I sing of a maiden
> That is makeles;
> King of all Kings
> To her son she ches.
>
> He came al so still
> There his mother lay,
> As dew in April
> That falleth on the spray.
>
> Mother and maiden
> Was never none but she;
> Well may such a lady
> Goddes mother be.
>
> Anon.

One of the two most powerful symbols of the Christian religion is of a baby in its mother's arms – Jesus in the arms of Mary. Probably no other theme has been painted so frequently by artists, and at Christmas, even now a potent festival in our secular culture, people still exchange cards showing this ancient image. Mary, whether shown in poverty, or in comfortable affluence, is always depicted as a loving and kindly mother, patient, gentle, often beautiful. Sometimes the baby sits on her lap, sometimes she cuddles it, or plays with it giving it fruit, sometimes she is feeding it at the breast. Always the sense is of peace, contentment, feminine grace and gentleness, with soft pleasing colours – blue, green, a deep red. Often there is a sense of timelessness or eternity.

Mary has been particularly treasured in the older Christian traditions, Orthodoxy and Catholicism. Their churches have many images of her, some of great beauty, some aesthetically vulgar, though often much loved. Some churches, such as Chartres Cathedral, are dedicated to the Virgin, and are full of imagery connected with her. At Chartres there are the great rose windows, the maze at the centre of the nave, the many windows depicting her, and two extraordinary statues, Notre Dame de Sous Terre and Notre Dame de Chartres. The second of these is an object of such devotion that it is common to see worshippers prostrating themselves before it. The first aroused such passions that during the French Revolution the mob dragged it out into the courtyard and set fire to it. In title and appearance the Madonnas, like the black madonnas in other parts of Europe, seem to reach back to a pagan past in which what was adored was the Earth Mother or the Earth itself.

Personally, I am very moved by this image of maternal love. In a world of extraordinary brutality, here, in the very heart of Christianity, is an image speaking to us of tenderness, of gentleness, of safety and of mutual loving. It speaks to us too of universal experience. Each one of us has only survived to the degree to which some other human being, almost always our mother, has fed, bathed, held and encouraged us. We might go further and suggest that our capacity to love others with some degree of mutuality derives from our parents, and more particularly, our mother's capacity to love us. That most, if not all, mothers find this difficult to do – that they fail to a greater or lesser degree – does not alter the huge importance of the attempt and the achievement, one that is mirrored in the pictures of Mary. The first weeks and months of life, and indeed the months in the womb beforehand, shape our capacity to love, and continue to comfort or distress us, at any rate to move us profoundly, for the rest of our lives. No wonder that worshippers fall to their knees before the Madonna de Sous Terre, or reverently kiss the foot of the tiny Virgin of Montsarrat in the Pyrenees. For they perceive that they are near to the very quick of life, to a source that feeds them even in middle age. It is part of the power of Christianity to find this source within itself, drawing upon earlier traditions and experiences of humankind. In utter simplicity it puts worshippers in touch with the springs of their own lives through the person of the universal mother Mary.

But Mary plays an ambiguous role within Catholicism, not part of the godhead, yet sometimes revered more than any of the persons of the Trinity. In a tiny village church in the Pyrenees I remember a medieval statue in which Mary sits with the infant Jesus on her lap. In his hands Jesus holds the book of the living and the dead, the book that decides who shall be saved and damned, but his mother holds her hands over his, making it impossible for him to open the book. Mary is 'soft-hearted', apparently more merciful than God.

For feminists Mary poses particular problems. The profound love and respect which Catholics have borne towards Mary is thought to have coloured attitudes to women, so that all women are thereby dignified. As recently as 1988 the Pope was begging Catholic women to take the Virgin Mary as their model (*Mulieris Dignitatem*). Yet no woman really can take the Virgin as her model (a very different thing from a symbol), since no other woman can conceive without sexual intercourse. 'Mother and maiden, Never none but she.'

There is an ironic footnote to all the recommendations to be like the Virgin. In March 1991 it emerged that many women, some of them virgins, were using modern science to try to become pregnant without the act of intercourse. The Roman Catholic Archbishop of Birmingham, among others, expressed shock at the idea of dissociating the birth of a child from the context of a committed relationship between husband and wife, saying that this was no way to bring a child into the world, an unconsciously comic observation in view of Christian history. Questions about the difficulties of being brought up in a one parent family were considered. Other questions about women's 'need' of men, and the deeper links this has with patriarchy, were not.

Nor is the submission of the Virgin at the moment when she is overshadowed by the Holy Spirit at the Annunciation necessarily a model for the way women should conduct themselves in other situations, though the Churches have repeatedly enjoined this kind of submission and obedience on women. The famous 'be it unto me according to thy word' response has been used to manipulate and control Christian women, to force them to agree with authorities with whom they should not agree by making submission a virtue.

Many men and women in Catholic and Orthodox countries pray to the Virgin, obviously comforted by a sense of the archetypal mother, Mary. In addition Mary often seems to make a particular appeal to those men who are living lives in which flesh and blood women play a minimal part. Thomas Merton, living in the all-male world of a Trappist monastery at Gethsemani, Kentucky, speaks of Mary in a way typical of many celibate priests. 'You take your rosary out of your pocket, and get in your place in the long file, and start swinging homeward along the road with your boots ringing on the asphalt and deep, deep peace in your heart! And on your lips, silently, over and over again, the name of the Queen of Heaven . . . "Hail Mary, full of grace, the Lord is with Thee . . .".'[32]

Yet there seems little evidence that general attitudes to women in Catholic countries are particularly caring. Because Mary is so pure, so chaste, so tied to the image of the mother (whom the child prefers to think of as not having sex with father), she is no sort of model for all the women who are sexually attractive and sexually responsive to men except to cast a sort of oblique slur on them. This flies in the face of commonsense – if women were universally chaste the human race would die out – yet some Christian statements seem to be pressing this impossible ideal upon women.

By the excessive emphasis on chastity Catholic cultures seem to emphasize its opposite – the work of the Irish writer James Joyce, for example, often depicts a tortured lust in which young men cease to see women as real people but only as relievers of the 'burning' of which St Paul wrote. Such women can be objects of pornography, can be prostituted or raped or beaten, perhaps as punishment for not being 'chaste' like Mary. Fantasies about 'the Magdalen' based, like fantasies about the Virgin herself, on only the slimmest biblical evidence, have always enticed the Catholic imagination. Yet the objects of the fantasy are often thought of with dread or contempt.

But no image that has worked as strongly in the human imagination as that of the Virgin Mary can be discarded or forgotten. In so many ways she is an immensely precious figure within the whole of Christian culture – 'humanizing' God in popular imagination in the sense of making him gentler and more understanding, humanizing us with the image of motherly tenderness and kindness.

It is a 'civilizing' influence that we need, that is of value so long as it is not allowed to stand alone as representing all that being a woman means, and so long as the Virgin is not used to trick women into 'obedient' behaviour.

It is as if, as we try to relate to men, a figure stands behind us and it is that figure to which men relate and not the real woman. Sometimes the figure is that of Eve – woman as dangerously seductive and treacherous – and she is treated with contempt. Sometimes the figure is one of supernatural dread, as with the witch or in the case of the Hindu goddess Kali, carrying her male scalps and severed penises (yet in life, as opposed to myth, men attack and mutilate women far more often than the other way round – an example of the inversion of the facts so common in male/female relations). Sometimes it is the figure of an impossibly virtuous and chaste woman, a sort of icon, with whom we can connect no more easily than with the other figures. But all three of these views held by men seem to merit exclusion, whether the exclusion of fear, the exclusion of shame, or the exclusion of adoration. Everyone of these stereotypes has been, and continues to be, used to limit and oppress women, to deny them education and work, opportunity and autonomy.

The least discussed attitude to women, and indeed the most difficult to discuss, is the attitude of fear. Whether we are speaking of the 'awe of the goddess' that afflicted ancient peoples, the terror of the Huli men that women may 'contaminate' their beds or their food, or the rigorous exclusion of women from many parts of our own society until recent times e.g. Oxbridge colleges, men's clubs, the priesthood, there is a sense of the irrational at work, of powerful taboos operating of which we are only partially aware. In the societies we are discussing, women have outwardly had almost no power. Men are not only physically stronger than they are, but they hold almost all the authoritative positions, as kings, leaders, soldiers, judges and priests. Yet the attitudes of the Huli or, initially, of all-male institutions asked to admit women, nearly always implies the opposite: the sense that women, even when denied any outward vestige of authority, are still powerful, dangerously so, and without rigorous supervision will be a threat to men. Their relegation to the domestic sphere, it is implied, is not a gross injustice but rather an establishment of a necessary balance of power.

Debarred so often from male religious ritual, women have had some rituals of their own, often associated with childbirth. A huge lore gathers around pregnancy and giving birth, much of it passed on orally – I remember my own pregnancies of thirty years ago, and the word being passed to me by older women about the sex of my unborn baby (divined from the position I carried it), about thinking 'good' thoughts to help my baby, and drinking raspberry-leaf tea to ease the labour. Compared to the immediate life and death importance of birth rituals, most male rituals, though clearly culturally important, look a little contrived. It is interesting to remember in this context that some of the objections to the ordination of women to the priesthood by men have been along the lines of '*You* can have babies. You should therefore let *us* be priests.'

Some of the fear of women may derive from the mysterious rituals of menstruation or birth, of which evidence is perceived and half understood by small boys. Blood, otherwise associated with injury, or death, may in itself be frightening, particularly when it belongs to a beloved mother. Fear may also pass swiftly into envy. Women alone can achieve the extraordinary creative act of giving birth, an act that has a miraculous quality even to the women themselves. All other creation – writing, painting, making music – pales into insignificance before producing actual living beings. Yet women are often mocked by men for their poor creative achievement.

The American psychologist Dorothy Dinnerstein produced a different theory for men's fear of women. In *The Rocking of the Cradle and the Ruling of the World*[33] she advances the theory that the fact that women are the almost universal nurturers of small children gives men a dread of their power that lasts for the rest of their lives. Men, like Alex Portnoy in Philip Roth's *Portnoy's Complaint*, who have felt frightened by their mothers in infancy for whatever reason – because their mothers bullied them, neglected them, suffered from mental illness, or simply seemed bigger and stronger than they were – grow up determined that never again will women hold power over them. Dorothy Dinnerstein's solution is that men should play a larger or equal part in caring for the young. Until a society attempts this solution we shall never know whether her ideas are correct, though the increasing part nowadays that many men play in caring for their children may begin to offer clues.

At a rational level Dorothy Dinnerstein's theory offers an interesting explanation, but so many of our feelings about our mothers, and so perhaps eventually about other women, are not rational. This huge caring figure at whose breast we feed, whose concern keeps us alive, whose love we crave, assumes for many of us, in the early years of life, a sort of luminosity that places an indelible imprint upon us. Like the goddesses who come and go in the pages of the Odyssey, comforting, advising and consoling, our mothers, initially, may be figures of mystical awe, who both delight and satisfy or frighten and savagely disappoint us. Whether the delight or the pain predominate may profoundly affect all future attitudes to women. In the case of little girls it affects not only their attitude to other women but also their attitude to themselves – if their mother is experienced as strong and happy then it is safe for them to emulate her example. If she is weak and timid the girl has difficulties. In the case of the little boy if the sense of delight in his mother predominates then he may look for that pleasure and delight again in other women. If fear and pain predominate then he may find himself avoiding women in intimate relationships, or seeking ways of dominating and controlling them. Buried in all this, even in our would-be rational society, is a sense of the initial encounter of the mother as being sacred – filled with awe – and primitive societies are much better than we are at portraying the power and glory of that vision of the feminine. Perhaps the sculptor Henry Moore has expressed it better than any other contemporary, with his great, glorious female figures planted as powerfully as trees.

Yet many men in many societies, and perhaps all men at times, clearly experience women as dangerous to them, feelings demonstrated in the symbol of the *vagina dentata*, the toothed vagina, only waiting for an unwary man to put his penis inside to bite it off. Male sexuality, with its proud symbol of the phallus, is more fragile than its female counterpart, securely lodged inside the body. Nor is it only a physical question. Since, for full sexual intercourse to take place, it is necessary for a man to achieve and sustain an erection, man is also vulnerable to psychological events – contempt, mockery, undermining remarks, indifference – that may in effect temporarily castrate him. Alex Portnoy remembers, among so many other humiliations, a hospital nurse who dealt with his unwanted erections in the examination room by a contemptuous flick of her finger.

Perhaps it is this double message from men – of a greater physical strength than women which is feared, on the one hand, and of a private vulnerability for which women secretly mock them on the other – which is so simply captured in *Yaaba*. An ancient arrangement by which women apparently hand over power to men – letting them strut in their rituals and huff and puff before their enemies, while retaining the power to destroy them in private – is not peculiar to Africa. All of us know it in the intricacies of complicated power plays, and our literature expounds it endlessly. The question is, with the growth of consciousness and understanding, can we not do better? Can we release men from their disabling fears of women, and women from the dishonesties of wielding power covertly? Can we escape from the rule of Kali?

Notes

1. Elizabeth Cady Stanton. *The Woman's Bible*, quoted by Ruth Page, 'Elizabeth Cady Stanton's *The Woman's Bible*', in Ann Loades, ed., *Feminist Theology: A Reader* (SPCK 1990), p. 18.
2. Clement of Alexandria, *Paidogogos*, II,33,2, quoted in Uta Ranke-Heinemann, *Eunuchs for Heaven*. Andre Deutsch 1990.
3. Peter Brown, *The Body and Society* (Faber and Faber 1989), pp. 168–9.
4. Thomas Aquinas. *Summa Theologiae: A Concise Translation*, Timothy McDermott, ed. (Eyre and Spottiswood 1990), p. 143.
5. Jerome, Letter xiv: To Asella, quoted by Karen Armstrong in *Gospel According to Woman* (Hamish Hamilton 1986), pp. 57–9.
6. Jerome, Letter cxvii. 4, quoted by Armstrong, ibid.
7. Ranke-Heinemann, p. 112.
8. Ranke-Heinemann, pp. 84–101.
9. St Bonaventure's *Life* of St Francis, ch. 4, 'Advancement of the Order', in E. Gurney Slater, tr., *The Little Flowers of St Francis* (Everyman 1963), pp. 331–2.
10. The Very Rev. John William Burgon, Dean of Chichester, 'To Educating Young Women like Young Men and with Young Men – a Thing Inexpedient and Immodest' (a sermon preached before the University of Oxford in the Chapel of New College on Trinity Sunday, 8 June 1884).
11. quoted by Armstrong, p. 100.
12. Armstrong, p. 115.
13. James Cowan, *Mysteries of the Dream-Time: The Spiritual Life of Australian Aborigines* (Prism Press 1989), pp. 5, 14, 17.
14. Cowan, p. 19.
15. William L. Countryman *Dirt, Greed and Sex* (SCM Press 1989), chs 2, 3.
16. Alyson Peberdy, 'Ritual and Power' in Monica Furlong, ed., *Mirror to the Church* (SPCK 1988), pp. 17–23.
17. Countryman, p. 253.
18. Christopher Wordsworth, Bishop of Lincoln, 'Christian Womanhood and Christian Sovereignty'.
19. see note 10.

20. quoted in Brian Heeney, *The Women's Movement in the Church of England 1850–1930* (Clarendon Press 1988), p. 18.
21. quoted in Heeney, p. 18.
22. Heeney, p. 19.
23. Heeney, p. 27.
24. Heeney, p. 87.
25. Heeney, p. 96.
26. Robert Runcie, Archbishop of Canterbury, speech to WCC at Sheffield, 1981.
27. quoted in Lawrence Stone, *The Family, Sex and Marriage in England*, abridged edition (Pelican Books 1979), p. 138.
28. Charles Lamb, 'Modern Gallantry', *Essays of Elia*, p. 109.
29. Maude Royden, *The Coming Day* (January 1916) 3, quoted in Sheila Fletcher, *Maude Royden* (Basil Blackwell 1989), p. 136.
30. Walter Scott, *Marmion*.
31. Virginia Woolf, *Three Guineas* (Hogarth Press 1938), p. 288
32. Thomas Merton, *The Seven Storey Mountain* (Harcourt Brace 1948; SPCK 1990), p. 393.
33. Dorothy Dinnerstein, *The Rocking of the Cradle and the Ruling of the World*. Women's Press 1987.

3. Woman in Her Own Eyes

The matter used for a priest is important. The priest needs to be a man to represent Jesus Christ, the God-man. Christ, the Word of God, the second person of the Blessed Trinity, took human form and was born as a man called Jesus. Neither an angel nor a woman could ever be a man. What a priest tells us is something not about the priest, but about God.

Margaret Hood, Women Against the Ordination of Women, *The Independent*, 15 December 1986

'You see I don't think much of my own sex, Mr. Hartright – which will you have, tea or coffee? – no woman does think much of her own sex, although few of them confess it as freely as I do.'

Wilkie Collins *The Woman in White* (Oxford University Press 1973), p. 26

I have no hesitation in declaring my full belief in the inferiority of woman, nor that she brought it upon herself . . . It was the woman who was the first to fall and to draw her husband into the same transgression. Thence her punishment of physical weakness and subordination. . . .'

Charlotte M. Yonge, *Womankind* (1876), British Library

MARIAN HALCOMBE, the speaker in the quotation from *The Woman in White*, is an intelligent, charming, loyal and remarkably brave woman who repeatedly feels obliged in conversation to denigrate not just herself but the entire female sex. 'Women can't draw – their minds are too flighty, and their eyes are too inattentive.'[1] She is a plain woman, and as such, in her Victorian upper-class milieu, unmarriageable, unlike her pretty half-sister Laura. But it is not only her plainness that troubles her. She feels obliged to make routine references to her stupidity and inferiority (though she is markedly superior in every way to her male guardian) and to other supposed weaknesses of women. Recalling Eve she makes an ironic remark about curiosity – she and the hero, Hartright, are trying to solve a mystery. 'Don't despair, Mr Hartright. This is a matter of curiosity; and you have got a woman for your ally. Under such conditions, success is certain, sooner or later.'[2]

Possibly Wilkie Collins means to make her continual self-deprecation a clue to her character – the character of a very intelligent woman with no real opportunity to use her abilities outside the home – but, as Marian Halcombe herself remarks of her contemporaries, 'No woman does think much of her own sex.'[3]

Women have come a long way since Marian Halcombe's day – it is possible to imagine her nowadays as a barrister or a senior civil servant – yet it is still possible to pick up the same lack of self-esteem in many modern women. Education helps, earning money helps, professional expertise helps, yet many of the old doubts linger among women. They are acutely sensitive to sneers and mockery – those ancient weapons of men when women are thought to be getting out of hand. When the word 'strident' is used (and it is often used of women mildly expressing an opinion), or 'aggressive' or 'unfeminine', women frequently shrink back in pain, fearful of taking on a conflict which puts them in such an unfavourable light.

Other women, who should be their allies, frequently withdraw at this point. How often have I heard women deacons disclaiming links with the Movement for the Ordination of Women (itself a very moderate organization) – 'Oh, I couldn't join them, they're so strident!' By such simple expedients can potential allies be separated and fruitful change blocked.

Behind the fear of stridency is a fear of ceasing to be appealingly feminine, of appearing masculine and so not being attractive to men. It often seems to me odd that many women will sacrifice so much in order to be attractive to men – it is a fundamental weakness in their struggles to get even elementary justice in the world – until I remember that men have represented authority in our culture and sexual attraction has often been women's only way of holding their own within the culture – Marian Halcombe's desperate situation, so different from that of her pretty sister, bears this out. So to give up claims to control men by sexual attraction feels like entering a battle without weapons. It takes extraordinary confidence to do it.

Each woman, by the time she is an adult, has had her inferiority reinforced in a thousand ways, to the point where she has taught herself to block out her awareness. 'I personally have never been discriminated against,' women often say at their first encounter with the women's movement, only gradually, and in enormous pain, recalling the comments by relatives and teachers, the assumptions in books and films, the whole pressure of the culture which drove the message home with such blanket coverage that it was almost unnoticeable. On a recent gardening programme I heard an interviewer say to a famous old gardener whom he was interviewing, 'You must have been terribly disappointed when you had a daughter.' Although the famous gardener, to his credit, stoutly denied that he was disappointed to have a child who was a girl (and who had become a professional gardener), neither party seemed to find the question odd.

The assumption in our society, as many observers have noted, is that to be male is the norm, and that to be a woman is to be divergent from this, to be Other. Many girls have endured the disappointment of their parents that they were not boys, often being told the male names already picked out before their births. Fathers sometimes seemed to feel as if begetting girls was a slight on their maleness. Mothers resented it because through bearing a boy they might have participated vicariously in male strength, might, in a sense, have experienced the supposed triumph of having a penis. The perceived advantages of male strength openly confirmed women's sense of deep inferiority – it is difficult to feel the equal of someone who can fell you with a blow – and easy to forget other strengths and abilities, especially when these are rarely affirmed by public acclamation. Where women were acclaimed it was, frequently, precisely for the weakness, dutifulness, sweetness and submission that their painful sense of inferiority imposed on them. When they were attacked and rebuked, it was precisely for their attempt to break free of these shackles, to be strong and independent. 'We love you so long as you remain prisoners' was the message, 'and oh, what beautiful, fascinating prisoners you are. Sing in your cages, and we will love you and take care of you. Sulk, and you will regret it. . . .'

The extraordinary determination and courage with which women, at least in part, have broken free of their cages is one of the most moving stories in all history. The brave eighteenth- and nineteenth-century women who began to dare to think in a new way, the epic struggle of the suffragists and suffragettes, the equally epic struggles for women to achieve university education and entrance to the professions, all began to spring the trap, the deadly blend of admiration, flattery, bullying and violence that had kept women subject before. Many different strands – the Enlightenment, the spread of education, middle-class economic prosperity, effective contraception – played a part in it. The change of heart undergone by some influential male writers – John Stuart Mill, Bernard Shaw, Bertrand Russell, the Bloomsbury group, among others – also influenced public ideas.

Yet as interesting as the courage of women who moved ahead and out of the female ghetto, is the terror of many women who could not make the transition, something little spoken about in feminist circles. The suffragettes had to contend against a kind of contra movement cobbled together by influential MPs, clergy and members of the House of Lords, composed of female friends and relatives who could be persuaded to say that their sex did not want, or need, the vote. Such a one was Lady Jersey, the vice-president of the National League for Opposing Women's Suffrage. A political hostess and *grande dame*, she interfered continually behind the scenes, writing to friends at the Foreign Office to suggest withholding passports from women who wished to initiate a peace conference in Holland, both publicly and secretly attacking well-known suffragists such as Maude Royden. As Maude Royden's biographer Sheila Fletcher remarked of Lady Jersey, 'One can see why (she) did not need a vote.'[2]

In our own time we have seen a rather similar, though less influential, organization spring up over the issue of women's ordination – Women Against the Ordination of Women.

It is fascinating to try to understand the psychology of those who work to try to lessen power and opportunities for people of their own kind, i.e. women. What is particularly striking is their way of distancing themselves from their embattled and struggling sisters, and the way they often look upon them with contempt. *They* are not struggling and powerless, *they* are not objects of male scorn and contempt. If they take sides it is with the men – 'look how good we are being', flattering male authority with the comforting placebos that *of course* they don't want the vote or ordination or anything else that may cause a moment's unease. Sometimes they follow this up with the arch claim that they have never had any difficulty in getting their own way, presumably by some devious method of sexual charm or flattery. There is a prize for their loyalty – male approval – and a name for their ploy, drawn from the life of slaves in America who, in much more pitiful circumstances, sometimes 'sucked up' to their male masters – 'Uncle Tom-ism', the perversion of toadyism and creeping adulation.

For every woman who joins an anti-woman organization, however, there are many more who feel faintly uncomfortable whenever the *status quo* is challenged, perhaps without ever knowing quite why. A lifetime's silent acquiescence to inferior status leaves a sediment of guilt, shame, and fear, and a horror of mockery. So long as the system remains unchallenged, however, the painful repressions can remain securely in place.

But as soon as women, braver, or less frightened than the rest, begin to ask the painful questions – 'Why don't women have the vote?', 'Why should women be deprived of higher education?', 'Why should women not be able to enter a profession?', 'Why should men control the means of contraception?', 'Why are women so badly paid for their work?', 'Why can women not be priests?', the predictable onslaught of male rage is released, and each woman begins to experience a great deal of remembered, but hitherto repressed, pain. Some move through this and join the campaigners. Others bitterly resent the action of those who have caused the old wounds to bleed, and continue to oppose and bad-mouth them for trying to change the status quo.

Thus, though all women know that the stereotype they are obliged to conform to does not fit them, any more than the tiny shoes of aristocratic Chinese women genuinely fitted their feet, women have colluded massively with male expectations of them. Only very gradually are numbers of women feeling free enough to try out styles of life for themselves, and ask new questions – 'Do we want to give birth, and bring up children?', 'Do we want all our life energy to be sacrificed upon the altar of the family?'. 'Why do men take so little responsibility for children, and women so much?' etc.

The questions are difficult questions to ask, taking women into uncharted waters. Not all experiments in new life-styles work out well, sometimes because they are misguided and foolish in the first place, sometimes because it is so hard to redesign ancient habits and expectations. Yet, as women begin to experience power and feel familiar with it, they become bolder in insisting upon their own wisdom and insights, and will not easily be forced back into old habits, damaging to women's health and happiness.

One way that anti-feminine conservatism in the churches operates is by speaking emotively of 'the Family'. To hear the advocates of the Family talk, you would imagine that until recent years all was sweetness and light, and most families were happy and content. Yet it was because the upkeep of the family was and is so often at women's expense, and women did not and often do not have a voice, that a sort of bogus security was and, to some extent, is maintained. The family has operated both to keep women imprisoned within the home, bound to its many duties, and also to maintain a particular kind of sexual order, a framework in which children could be reared. A framework is itself a good thing, and when it works well the family is a fine way to relieve human loneliness, to comfort sexual need, to offer both parents and children some stability and emotional security. Yet behind many church pronouncements about the family, and more particularly about other forms of 'family', which do not keep the traditional rules – single parent families, households of women and children, homosexual households, etc. – it is possible to note a will to power and to sexual control. Pronouncements appear less interested in making people happy and satisfied than in making sure that sexuality measures up to an approved (Christian) standard of traditional family life. But 'Christian' family life as we have known it was not only very costly for women, as well as encouraging a certain detachment in many men, it also failed to meet the emotional needs of large numbers of the population. Returning to it is not a particularly desirable option, though modified forms of it might be liberating for women and for many others.

Masochism

One way women have dealt with their inferior status has been by taking a masochistic position over against male sadism. Masochism is often a submission technique from those who despair of receiving 'love' or at any rate, attention, by any other means. Life only becomes tolerable by identifying with a stronger partner and subordinating one's own wishes entirely to those of the partner. Masochism is marked by its submissiveness, by its pleas (guaranteed to invoke sadistic responses), by its general 'pardon me for breathing' approach. One of the shocks of recent surveys is the discovery of how frequently women, on all levels of society, get beaten by their husbands/male partners – some think in as many as one in ten relationships – and how serious some of the resultant injuries can be (see Chapter 6). It is interesting to employ the sadism/masochism model in examining the way the process of legislation for women's ordination in the Church of England has gone forward. I am thinking of the endless pleas curtly dismissed, the continual disappointments as promises were broken and agreed courses of action were delayed, the overt sadism of some of the speeches in Synod. It takes two to play the sadism/masochism game, of course, and it is a notoriously difficult habit to step out of. Yet at least some of the women involved worked their way to a new position, discovering that the much vaunted Christian method of 'patience and longsuffering', so far as women were concerned, only led into a new round of the game of frustration. The most useful method seemed to be a paradoxical one of both getting tougher and simultaneously losing interest, so that there was no one left to take another beating.

If masochism is one of the most frequently noted of women's reactions to their inferior status, then depression is its rival and sometimes companion. Two characters in recent drama – Lionel's neglected wife in David Hare's play *Racing Demon* and the pitiful alcoholic clergy wife in Alan Bennett's *Bed Among the Lentils*, one of the monologues in *Talking Heads* – both show clergy wives as deeply sad, lonely, lacking in all self-esteem. That so many Christians found these women recognizable should be a cause for concern.

'Geoffrey brings it up at the slightest pretext. "My wife's an alcoholic, you know. Yes. It's a great challenge to me and the parish as extended family." From being a fly in the ointment I find myself transformed into a feather in his cap. Included it in his sermon on Prayers Answered when he reveals that he and the fan club have been having these jolly get togethers in which they'd all prayed over what he calls "my problem". It practically sent me racing back to the Tio Pepe even to think of it.'[5]

Geoffrey's wife Susan is sunk in a desperate depression which she relieves first by alcohol, then, with more positive results, by going to bed with Mr Ramesh Ramesh, the Asian grocer, who points out to her that she would be nicer if she was not always drunk, thus precipitating the cure that Geoffrey publicly claims to be due to his love and prayers.

Susan is neglected and exasperated by a gaggle of other women in the parish who seek Geoffrey's attention and heap praise upon him, treating Susan as a nuisance and a rival. Depression, though by no means exclusive to women, is a common female malady, its passive anger suiting those of subordinate status.

Depression, breakdown, or other forms of invalidism are a familiar form of feminine protest. (The Victorian woman lying on a sofa with some unspecified malady but usually nursing a headache, feelings of weakness, faintness, and exhaustion, was an earlier expression of the tranquillized, sleeping-pill taking, unable-to-cope woman of today.) The hallmark of such maladies is their indirectness, their lack of confrontativeness, their passive-aggressive now-you-see-it-now-you-don't quality. By a depressive breakdown a woman is able to appear outwardly loyal to her husband while secretly attacking and seceding from him. Barbara, the wife in *Racing Demon*, puts up silently with only seeing her husband when he is exhausted, with the lack of sexual affirmation, with the long hours of loneliness succeeded by sudden demands to provide meals for all comers at improbable hours. Then she has a stroke. A silent revenge? Maybe, but if so it is one which damages her more than it damages her amiable, unseeing husband.[6] Similarly with Susan in *Bed Among the Lentils*. When she disgraces her husband with her drunkenness and inability to cope (before he cleverly turns her into a feather in his cap) it is *her* body and brain that is destroyed by alcohol and her self-esteem that suffers the pain of condescension from the patronizing parish.

The suffering of women is a favourite Christian refrain, from the implication from Genesis that women *ought* to suffer in childbirth, to the faintly pornographic paintings of women martyrs so common in Latin countries – St Agatha with her amputated breasts on a dish, St Catherine with her wheel – and the sermons in which, even nowadays, clergy single out women as those who should endure suffering with particular patience.

A few months ago, staying in the country in Wales, I went to a hymn-singing evening at the village church. For two verses of the hymns on the programme women, 'the ladies', were invited to sing alone. One was the verse from 'Rock of Ages' which goes:

> Nothing in my hand I bring,
> Simply to Thy Cross I cling;
> Naked, come to Thee for dress;
> Helpless, look to Thee for grace;
> Foul, I to the Fountain fly;
> Wash me, Saviour, or I die.

The other, from 'Come Down, O Love Divine', went:

> Let holy charity
> Mine outward vesture be,
> And lowliness become mine inner clothing.
> True lowliness of heart,
> Which takes the humbler part,
> And o'er its own shortcomings weeps with
> loathing.

I am sure that the Vicar meant, as they say, 'no harm', but the choice of these two verses as being especially appropriate for women to sing was fascinating in its indication of his unconscious assumptions and also in the attitudes it attempted to reinforce among women. Leaving out the possible prurience of 'Naked, come to thee for dress', the implication is that women are basically helpless, dirty and sinful, and that because of all these drawbacks it behoves them to remain in a humble and pleading role.

Women have internalized this belief all too successfully. Even in the movement for ordination itself the concept of women's suffering crops up repeatedly, women unwisely using their suffering as a weapon to plead for inclusion. I remember a woman speaker at a MOW Conference only a few years ago telling us that it was our duty to suffer: 'You will all have to suffer much much more before you get what you want.'

Behind this, I believe, is not only a secret sado-masochistic excitement at the thought of women's suffering, shared by both women and men, but also an odd Christian conviction, not entirely borne out in women's case by the facts, that , if you suffer enough, some privilege, some kind of respect, will be accorded to you – that, in fact, suffering will convey some vestigial power of control upon you. (Many men brought up by invalid mothers will testify how real that control could be on occasions – a control not of direct power but of guilt).

Flatter Them

The hopeless preoccupation with suffering has parallels with another secret agenda of women which often emerges when women's status is being discussed – the idea that it is possible to control men covertly by way of admiration, flattery, sexual charm, appealing helplessness, tears. Thus, no doubt, in the era of slavery, slaves learned that it was possible to ameliorate their fate. Sensitive consciences absolve the faint dishonesty in the practice by reflecting that women were ever thus, that in fact, it is the only way to get by, a fact of life forced upon one by circumstance. What is rarely brooded upon is the depth of oppression out of which such a solution springs.

Of course, for dependent personalities there are attractions in helplessness. If father or husband tells me what to do then I can do it with a convenient abrogation of responsibility for what is done. As his representative, not a full person in my own right, I cannot be blamed. (Generations of women have rebuked tradesmen, refused unwelcome invitations, or controlled their children by reference to the authority figure behind the scenes. 'My husband/your father doesn't/ wouldn't like it/let me.') In the church where the person of Father hovers over us in the person of God the Father, and is represented by the male Father-priest, we have a similar temptation to abrogate the worrying responsibility for our moral choices and simply do what we are told. Both men and women are in this position in the churches, but for women this double authority is particularly powerful because it mirrors their traditional situation in the family.

The Indian Rope Trick

Other women deal with the awkwardness of being women by a kind of Indian rope trick technique. It is often humiliating and uncomfortable to be a woman? Very well then, I will cease to be a woman, at least in some part of my own mind. I will become an honorary man. In the words of one woman I know (and I have a feeling I once uttered the very same words myself), 'I don't particularly think of myself as a woman.' She is a woman who got a Double First at Cambridge and who knows very well that her brain is much better than that of many men. But instead of proudly claiming the inheritance of very intelligent women as her own birthright she has tried to move into a less threatening position which is somehow beyond gender. This might be all right if one did not have a sneaking suspicion that she is ashamed of the feminine part of her, which excludes her from the citadels of male intelligence, or that she is perhaps nervous of inhabiting the role, said to be threatening to men, of Clever Woman. Somehow she has evaded the identification and solidarity which might have strengthened the status and esteem of her sisters. Like a black person who can 'pass for white', and does so, she has committed some secret and subtle form of betrayal.

Not all women make this betrayal by means of the intellect. Some are obsessed with physical strength and an exaggerated athleticism, some feel a need to dress as men down to purchasing shirts and trousers at male tailors, some have a need to pursue male skills and hobbies. There may be good reasons for such choices – women have often cultivated an unnecessary physical frailty, it might be important for them to learn more of the art of self-defence, male dress (or trousers at least) is often more suited to active pursuits, and women have been unnecessarily excluded from jobs and hobbies that they might have enjoyed.

It is not what women do that is suspect – I see no reason that they, like men, should not live, dress, work as they please – but the possible inner state of trying to escape from the 'shame' of being woman into the safer and more acceptable state of being male. Many, if not all, girls at some time in their growing. up play with and act out a male identity alongside their female one, but a male identity is not ultimately accessible to them and is destructive to themselves and others, if it is an indication of contempt for what is female, a refusal to join what has been seen, probably early in life, as the losing side.

Yet other women deal with the whole issue by not dealing with it at all, rejecting their femaleness by subtle means – neglecting their appearance, putting on weight or losing it – as if they are trying to live invisibly, or in a space where they can be excused the uncomfortable necessity of assuming their female identity or of stimulating male fantasy. Some Christian women who might have been role models for other women have this disturbing aura of having abdicated from their sexuality – I think of a woman like Evelyn Underhill – as if the duality buried in much Christian thinking has caused them to vacate their own womanliness. 'I'm not a sexual being, oh dear me, no!'

It is only now, a couple of generations on from the suffragettes, when so many gains have been made in freedom and opportunities for women, that we can begin to note women's various dodges to make their lot bearable. They have left undone those things that they ought to have done, and they have done those things that they ought not to have done, and what strikes us about it now, as women try to help one another to move into a fuller life, is how sadly life-denying many of the strategies were, life-denying not only for women and their daughters, but also for the men they loved and the boys they reared. Like all repressions those that have afflicted women are extraordinarily difficult to discover and to give up and we still have a long way to go in catching ourselves out.

But the outline of recovery is fairly clear. It is to choose plain speaking, direct anger, confrontation, action, rather than depression, silence, passive acceptance, drugs, alcohol, invalidism and violence. It is to ask for what we want and need, and see that, within reasonable limits, we get it. It is to reject suffering wherever we can (it comes to us soon enough without our going out of our way to select it), and to inform clerics and others that that is not our programme. It is to reject false pictures and stereotypes of women as irrelevant to us and reserve for ourselves the freedom to be the sort of women we wish to be. It is to reject words of oppression – 'strident', 'aggressive', 'unfeminine' – and not to side with those who use them against other women. It is to take responsibility for ourselves and not take refuge behind authority figures. It is to struggle to work through our dependence – both men and women can help us to do this – to have an ideal of growing female strength, courage and resourcefulness. It is a discovery of self-esteem.

Most important of all it is to take pleasure in being women, as we begin to discern for the first time what that might mean, to admire and support other women, to be glad to be who we are and what we are and to be it for all we are worth. If this provokes scorn, ridicule, contempt, then this should not cause us to deviate from our course.

There are times, looking at women's situation, more particularly within the Church, when it seems problematic whether women really want change, whether, slave-like, they are not gravely tempted to keep everything the way it is because it is less frightening, less demanding.

So far as the ordination issue is concerned there is little doubt that the Church of England could not maintain its antipathetic stance for more than a month or two if women decide to move out of their passivity and demand a very different status. (The very word 'status' is often alarming to Christian women, a fact skilfully exploited by those opposed to women's ordination who often ask how women can be so crass and unchristian as to require status. But what is wrong with status? Most bishops and clergy seem to bear with it cheerily enough.) The official figures for the mean average of women in church congregations is sixty per cent. A look round most church congregations would suggest that the active churchgoing figure is much higher than that.[7] Sixty per cent, or more, who took their own position as women seriously and who grasped the importance of doing so not just for themselves but for the general wellbeing of women in a society where many women are gravely abused, could make a considerable difference, could transform Christian attitudes.

Sometimes it appears as if women's stake in being oppressed is too attractive to them for them to surrender it in favour of effective change. Self-pity is terribly seductive (particularly sometimes in feminist circles) but it rots resolve, and fear takes away the appetite for attempting new things. A kind of dread – that Father will be antagonized without the bid for freedom being successful – invades us, and we are tempted to listen to the anodynes of those who plead the need for time, for patience, for some mysterious movement of the Spirit that will make everything much clearer (but where can this movement happen except in us?). At such moments the new life for the Church that the women's movement within it so abundantly promises is in danger of being aborted – the sheer weight of the Church and the toxicity of its terror becomes total threat.

Yet unwanted and unsung, cold in its bare manger, the new birth is taking place, and those of us, women and men, who have some inkling of it, can assist at it, or drive it from the inn. It is here, here, here, we cry, like the ox and the ass in medieval carols. The simple (like the shepherds), and the wise (like the magi), know what it is they see.

Notes

1. Wilkie Collins, *The Woman in White* (1860; Oxford University Press 1973), p. 28.
2. Collins, p. 40.

3. Collins, p. 26.
4. Sheila Fletcher, *Maude Royden: A Life* (Blackwell 1989), pp. 123–4.
5. Alan Bennett, *Talking Heads* (Faber 1988), p. 40.
6. David Hare, *Racing Demon*. Faber 1990.
7. Working Group appointed by the Standing Committee of the General Synod of the Church of England, *Servants of the Lord: Roles of Women and Men in the Church of the England*, Section 11.

4 · Figures of Speech

*Do you use inclusive
language in your
services?*

*No, inclusiveness
is so very
divisive!*

'Dear God, are boys really better than girls? I know you are one, but try to be fair.'

Eight-year-old girl in *Children's Letters to God*, Collins 1967

God the Father is not a 'male' deity . . . When we reflect upon our addressing God as 'our Father' we soon realize that no sexuality is implied in God . . . To intrude into the biblical portrait of the eternal Father, the incarnate Son and the adopted sons (male and female) the further picture of God as mother or God as parent is to distort the whole fine balance of the content of revelation. It is to introduce sexuality where none was intended . . .

Graham Leonard, Iain MacKenzie, Peter Toon, *Let God be God* (Darton, Longman and Todd 1989), pp. 55–6.

The first thing to be said of course is that Hagia Sophia is God Himself. God is not only Father but a Mother. He is both at the same time, and it is the 'feminine aspect' or Feminine principle in the divinity that is the Hagia Sophia. But of course as soon as you say this the whole thing becomes misleading: a division of an 'abstract' divinity into two abstract principles. Nevertheless, to ignore this distinction is to lose touch with the fullness of God. This is a very ancient intuition of reality which goes back to the oldest Oriental thought . . . . For the 'masculine – feminine' relationship is basic in all reality – simply because all reality mirrors the reality of God.

Thomas Merton, letter to Victor Hammer, 14 May 1959 (Thomas Merton Studies Center, Kentucky)

We live, and are formed as human beings, in a civilization in which qualities regarded as 'feminine' are disvalued in relation to qualities regarded as 'masculine', and in which men have predominance over women. To name and depict God almost exclusively in male terms reinforces those distinctions, since it suggests that women are unfit, or less fit than men, to represent the beauty and greatness of God in language.

Brian Wren, *What Language shall I Borrow?* (SCM Press 1989), p. 3.

Since God is male, the male is God.

Mary Daly, *Beyond God the Father* (Boston: Beacon Press 1973; Women's Press 1986)

AFTER THE QUESTION of ordination itself nothing, except perhaps homosexuality, is liable to get General Synod or a smaller gathering of Christians so incensed and unhappy as a discussion of 'inclusive language' – the attempt to shift the liturgical language of the Church away from its present strong gender-bias. Language, like the subject of homo-sexuality, touches every one of us at a point where we are vulnerable. Janet Morley who, together with Hannah Ward, published an early book of inclusive prayers, *Celebrating Women*,[1] in 1986 notes the contradiction evident in the angry expostulations. 'A feature of the response to pressure for inclusive language is the paradoxical insistence that, on the one hand, the issue is too trivial to be discussed and, on the other, that to raise it is positively satanic.'[2]

The force of the response suggests that, within the 'hold-all' term of 'inclusive language', something immensely important is being talked about, or perhaps a number of different things. As with other issues which concern women there is sometimes the feeling that the rational argument being put forward by opponents is not the real one, but a cover for something the speaker is not prepared to examine, at least in public. Thus objections are sometimes raised to inclusive language on aesthetic grounds, or nostalgic grounds, in so far as certain prayers and hymns and carols famous for centuries, or loved since childhood, are deeply loved by Christians. Of course issues of aestheticism and nostalgia – the beauty and associations of language – are important, and feminists no more than anyone else should ride roughshod over sensibilities. Where changes are clumsy, intrusive or silly it is possible for even ardent feminists to object – I am told that in a Christmas liturgy the words 'Behold the handperson of the Lord' were used – but there is no intrinsic reason why inclusive language cannot be sane, sensible, relevant and sensitive to aesthetic issues. Indeed the work of a number of feminist groups who write their own liturgies – the WIT Liturgy Group, the St Mark's Group at Wimbledon, the St Hilda Community and others up and down the country – show that it can be so.

But aestheticism, important as it is, is not the primary issue here. Far more important, and the reason that inclusive language has become such an important issue for many Christian women, is that exclusive language all too clearly mirrors women's centuries of invisibility and silence in the churches. Like the issue of ordaining women, a change in language indicates whether the change in church attitudes to women goes 'all the way through' or is merely cosmetic. To this extent it is a political, as well as a theological matter.

There are at least two major issues around inclusive language. The first of these is the way in which we think and talk about God. Although there are rare instances in which Anselm or Julian of Norwich speaks about God as mother, or of God taking us to the breast to feed us, the predominating images of God, many of them drawn from the Bible, are masculine images – God as soldier and general, as powerful, indeed almighty, as king/emperor, as judge. God is almost invariably referred to as 'he', even in contexts where he is depicted as enacting what, in traditional human terms, are 'female' tasks – feeding at the breast, mothering babies and the very young. In an attempt to accommodate this bizarre picture of a male God aping female functions, without allowing any implication that God might be as much (or as little) female as male, some theologians have invented a phrase about God as a 'mothering father'.

A tougher line is taken by Graham Leonard in *Let God be God*, written with Iain MacKenzie and Peter Toon.[3] To Bishop Leonard God *is* male in some very definite sense, though he insists that God is non-sexual and (although called Father, and referring to Jesus as his son) is not a parent. It is difficult to picture how, without the potential for sex or parenthood, God can be male in any sense that we understand the word, but, says the Bishop, 'God the Father is not a "male" deity.' Women, according to Leonard, should not

feel excluded since this God 'who is never called Mother'
has 'the best female qualities'. Now, although the Bible is a
very patriarchal document and certainly prefers male imagery for God, unfortunately for Leonard's argument it *does*
sometimes do what he says cannot be done and describe God
as female. Leonard has the answer to that, though. Whereas
God *is* male, *tout simple*, images in which God is shown as
female are only 'a simile'. There is something very strange,
and rather desperate, about this reasoning, and it has a
deeply defensive note to it.

For to change our way of talking and thinking about God
to include the female and, by implication, the sexual, would,
for the Bishop, undermine and destroy the Christian faith.
(The title of the book *Let God be God* is intended to convey
this threat as the title of William Oddie's book *What Will
Happen to God?* conveys it more clearly. It seems odd that
both of these intelligent men apparently believe that God is
in danger of being toppled by a bunch of women. Whatever
has become of his all-powerfulness?)

The theory of God as 'non-sexual' also seems to need some
examination. If human beings are 'made in the image of
God', and human creativity is inextricably linked with sexuality, both in conceiving new life, and in aesthetic concep-
tion, is it not possible that God's creativity is sexual in
some more comprehensive sense, and that maleness and
femaleness both derive from a divine act of intercourse which
brings the world into being? Why does Leonard *want* God
to be non-sexual? Many mystics – St Teresa and St John of
the Cross immediately come to mind – seem to experience
God as magnificently erotic. And where does human erotic
delight come from if not from God?

Anyway, whatever the sexuality, or lack of it, of God, it
is masculine language for God that has become the commonplace for those of us who have grown up in the Church, or
been converted to it – hearing over and over again, in hymns,
in prayers, in Bible readings, that God is a male God and
that he had a male Son. Those with a Catholic or Orthodox
slant to their religion are, of course, taught that the mother

of Jesus is of great importance, but not that she is part of the godhead.

Mary is, of course, a very significant figure in Christianity, yet for women and girls, not to mention men and boys, who attend most churches, Catholic, Orthodox or Protestant, the message of the male God and his male son is overwhelmingly there, Sunday after Sunday, reflected universally until very recently in the male faces and voices that speak from pulpit and altar. The Christian religion, the symbolism tells us, is about powerful male servants of a powerful male God, and women are admitted to this religion in a subordinate role as passive participants. (I remember a woman I met in Australia, the daughter, and granddaughter, and now the sister, of a priest, telling me of her sudden realization as she sat in church at the age of five that she would never be able to be a server like her brother. She wept.)

In painting, and on crucifix and statue, as well as in the person of male priests and ministers, a statement was silently being reiterated about women's role within Christianity, that was then further articulated in liturgical speech. The language of the prayers, with the emphasis on the male God and his male Son, the use of 'man', (apparently meaning both men and women), and on 'he' (apparently meaning both he and she) declared women's invisibility. Of course, the churches are not alone in employing such language – in recent memory it has been the unchallenged language of our society – but since Christianity largely shaped Western culture, literature and language, responsibility cannot easily be shifted. The Christian relegation of women, and the invisible role they have played in the liturgy (as in many other areas of Western society) is accurately reflected in liturgical language. Or, as it says so rightly in the Preface to the Alternative Service Book, 'Christians are formed by the way in which they pray, and the way they choose to pray expresses what they are.'[4]

One of the puzzling things about the opponents of inclusive language is that believing that, although Christians often address God as male, God is not 'really' male, they seem disproportionally upset when a female metaphor is used for

God, and seem to feel that this must imply that God is *really* female. Leonard makes the very puzzling suggestion that calling God 'Mother' has sexual connotations which calling God 'Father' does not have. William Oddie goes on to attribute goddess-worship, dancing in sacred groves, and all manner of strange carryings-on to Christian feminists who are attempting to use feminine imagery for God in the same way as masculine imagery has repeatedly been used. Perhaps certain minds get a thrill from pagan fantasies about women. Alas, the truth is duller: we have yet to establish a sacred grove.

Surely the truth must be that we say that God is 'like' men or 'like' women, because our minds are so formed that we need images; if we do not despise women we find no more problems in likening God to them than in likening God to men. Only if we find women somehow degraded, obscene, or inextricably connected to the baser elements of our humanity (as some men, and, tragically, some women seem to do), is it offensive to link them with the idea of God.

Of course, God is 'actually' neither a man nor a woman. Our ways of referring to God, however hallowed by tradition and sacred use, are little more than shorthand, or sketches, or initials, or mnemonics, for something, someone, very imperfectly understood by us, but far too important to be left out of our calculations.

For many years I think it was possible for women to live with a certain ambiguity in their sense of God, to see all these male images and male priests, to use the male-centred language, and yet somehow keep a sense of themselves as vital to the Christian religion (as dear to God, you might say) as any man. Perhaps we imagined that, whatever was being said, the churches believed that God was neither male nor female, and that women were valued as much as men. Some women still claim to be unmoved by the contradictions, but others of us now feel that we were extraordinarily naive, or perhaps more truly, part of a desperate process of denial.

Yet as women in many parts of the world began to ask

questions about their absence from pictures of the godhead, from priesthood, and from the more visible forms of ministry, and their invisibility from the language, the anger and vehemence of the male replies became unexpectedly revealing. In the first place, by a process of projection, women who asked such questions were widely condemned as 'strident and aggressive'. (It was interesting that when Mrs Kathleen Young was ordained priest in Ireland, in June 1990, her bishop, Dr Samuel Poyntz, felt a need to say that she was not 'an aggressive feminist in any way'.[5] No one had suggested that she was.)

In the second place, it was made clear to women that they caused enormous offence by simply asking the questions. Many men, and particularly many clergy, in the churches, who were dedicated to issues of justice, racial harmony, to women's emancipation and even, in some cases, to women's ordination, were deeply upset at the suggestion that female imagery might be used for God, or that liturgical language might be modified to make women feel more 'included'. It suggested that even if male sympathy could survive the Scylla of women's ordination (and in many cases it could not) then it tended to founder on the Charybdis of any suggestion that the female was at least as godlike as the male, or that women were equally included.

An interesting *cause célèbre* was that of the sculpture 'Christa' by Edwina Sandys exhibited in the Cathedral of St John the Divine in New York in 1981. This showed a woman wearing a crown of thorns and nailed upon a cross in exactly the same pose as a million paintings since the first century had shown Jesus Christ.

It was a novel idea, but not, one might think, a theologically improper one since the doctrine of the incarnation holds that Jesus in his death was entering into, and transforming, the suffering of all humankind, women as well as men. In a somewhat similar way African artists depict a black Christ, not because they necessarily imagine that the skin of Jesus was as dark as that of a tribesman from Central Africa, but because they recognize the kind of symbolic identification involved.

Yet the suggestion that God is neither male nor female, but that, if we are going to use human metaphors for God at all, it is equally possible to describe him/her in either male or female terms caused interesting offence. The Edwina Sandys sculpture was vilified, and attempts were made to deface it. Yet surely, to imply that woman is not 'on the cross' exactly as man is, is theologically dangerous (as well as childishly literal). For if woman is *not* included on equal terms in the dying and resurrection, that is to say the Easter transformation undergone by God and man, then she has no reason to be part of the Christian religion at all. It offers her nothing.

Behind the attacks on feminist ideas is often a kind of assumption of men as a 'master race' who must be permitted a monopoly in God. Like Graham Leonard, William Oddie believes that the 'masculine' God is essential to the survival of Christianity. In *What Will Happen to God*? he puts forward as 'evidence' of the maleness of God references in the Old Testament to God as 'like a father' and in the New Testament to God as a 'begetter', the begetter of a Son, Jesus.[6] In fact he feels God *must* be male in order to 'beget' all the rest of us as spiritual sons and daughters. He also makes abundant use of Jesus's prayers to his 'father', and his use of 'Abba' (Daddy) as a vocative. It is not merely that there is no place in Oddie's theology for female metaphors for God, it is also that there is a very limited understanding of metaphor itself.

Part of the tragedy of the debate about inclusive language, part of the tragedy of contemporary Christianity, is its literalness, its lack of a 'subtle understanding' of God, of religion, or of men and women. A subtle understanding has to do with a grasp of metaphor, that is to say, a poetic approach to the world. Joseph Campbell, an American writer with a vast knowledge of religious ritual, put it like this:

> A metaphor is an image that suggests something else. For instance, if I say to a person 'You are a nut' I'm not suggesting that I think the person is literally a nut. 'Nut' is a metaphor. The reference of the metaphor in religious traditions is to something transcendent that is not literally any thing. If you think that

the metaphor is itself the reference, it would be like going to a restaurant, asking for the menu, seeing beefsteak written there, and starting to eat the menu . . . every religion is true when understood metaphorically.[7]

The damage of the male metaphors has been done – the damage that back at the very roots of Christian thinking women were downgraded as being less godlike than men, and have been forced to carry the stigma of inferiority ever since. In countless ways the churches have enforced that degradation, silencing, ignoring, misunderstanding women, in some cases even forcing them to receive Communion after men, or to stay away from the altar because they were 'unclean'.

Exactly as one would expect, the use of language has expressed, promoted and reinforced that exclusion of women. Every little girl grows up learning that when a writer says 'he' a writer may mean both men and women, or may only mean men, and that it is up to her to acquire the taxing, and slightly humiliating, skill of being able to tell the difference. I can still remember feeling quite clever as a little girl when I learned this quirk of my mother tongue, of actually feeling pride in this perverse accomplishment as I felt pride in mastering punctuation or learning to tell the time, and even a sort of gratitude ('They *do* mean me after all'). Sometimes, when the issue of inclusive language comes up, one still hears older Christian women say, in baffled tones, 'But everyone knows that when it says "he" it means "she"' as if the old pride in repressing doubt and anger is still at work.

It is only fair to add that at an earlier stage of the development of English the word 'man' more genuinely represented both men and women than it does today, though this may also reflect the extent to which women were seen as more subsidiary to men, almost as if they had no separate existence of their own. To make this point *Making Women Visible*[8] includes two quotations 'Wit twa men (Simeon and Anna) that him comly grette' (1325), and 'The Lord had but one paire of men (Adam and Eve) in Paradise' (1597), a usage that would seem very odd today.

Unlike punctuation or spelling, this strangely complicated linguistic trick performs the extra function of instructing women in their social role, a role in which their experience and identity was to be swallowed up and lost sight of in the masculine (godlike) role.

The linguistic trick was comprehensively employed in the English language and in most European languages, and, of course, in liturgical language – the language of the Church. In England, where a vernacular language has been employed in the liturgy of the Church of England for hundreds of years, on every page, in every prayer and canticle, God is referred to as 'he', and is portrayed in almost exclusively male images – king, general, etc. Rather like black people in missionary churches forced always to believe in a God who, at least in many representations, appeared to be white, so women were forced always to understand a God who was entirely 'other' than them, or rather, since God and men were the norms, to recognize themselves as 'others' who could never hope to identify. All the same they were expected to do so. Even in baptism, and in the baptism prayers often echoed at confirmation – two rites which are surely intended to be about claiming an identity – women were enjoined to 'fight manfully', and to be 'a soldier and servant'. No crasser example of Christianity's blindness towards women could be found. In societies where women never fought in armies or became soldiers (except in disguise), and could not be 'manful' without doing damage to their own essential nature, they were required, in two of the most precious stages of the Christian life, to pretend, to misrepresent, to do violence to their own nature and life experience.

Behind this is male superiority by association. If God is male then men must be better than women. 'Since God is Male, the male is God' as Mary Daly puts it.[9] Follow this with the exclusion of references to women, female pronouns, female imagery, even female vocatives in Church, and the woman is reduced to a religious nonentity. (The last problem was recognised, ahead of time, by a well-known Victorian Anglo-Catholic priest, R.S. Hawker of Morwenstow in

Devon. Sharing Matins day by day with a congregation consisting only of his wife, he substituted 'Dearly beloved Charlotte' for 'Dearly beloved brethren'.)

There are other more obscure but relevant ways of excluding women: for example, in the ASB, fewer women than men find their way on to the calendar of saints (only a seventh as many), and those tend to be described in terms of their sexuality, as 'virgin', 'wife and mother', etc., whereas in the case of male saints it is not mentioned: certain Bible readings that give particular importance to women are truncated or omitted from the lectionary.[10]

For at least ten years now the issue of 'exclusive' and 'inclusive' language has been debated in Christian circles. As long ago as 1981 the Canadian Church brought out *Bad Language in Church*,[11] which discussed these issues, arousing a lot of interest in the press. In 1985 a Standing Committee of General Synod noted inclusive language as an issue which needed to be further explored. The Liturgical Commission of 1981–85 sought to be 'sensitive' about sexism in adapting material published for Rite B. There was good reason to be sensitive since the *Alternative Service Book 1980* had seemed blissfully unaware of the problem, though we know from Mrs Jean Mayland that it was brought to their attention.

However, a sense that, far from just 'going away', the issue was arousing more and more controversy caused General Synod in 1985 to set up the Commission on the subject which published a report in 1988: *Making Women Visible: Inclusive Language for use with the Alternative Service Book*. It was a curious title to sum up the work of a Commission on which, initially, there were thirteen men, plus a male chairman (the Bishop of Winchester) a male consultant and secretary, and only two women. (When one of the men resigned in September 1987, another woman was appointed.) Nor did the appearance of the report give much assurance when it came out, printed in dove grey and sugar pink, with the word 'Women' looking as if scrawled in lipstick across the cover.

In slightly acidic tones the commission discussed the issue of inclusive language, but admitted the depth of the conflict.

Sexist language causes great offence to some; others are deeply irritated at attempts to tamper with traditional texts and resonances. The complexity of the issues is less widely recognized. . . . 'Womankind', like 'humankind' is not a modern invention nor the product of an allegedly strident feminism. 'Man' is ambiguous, referring to a male, to a human being or to the human race depending on the context. The quotation from Loren Eiseley [see the beginning of this chapter] shows that the writer has been seduced by the ambiguity into understanding generic 'man' as male . . . . Used with the article, 'man' may increasingly be heard as male.[12]

While not prepared to change the wording of the creeds, the Commission while 'not of one mind on which changes are necessary or helpful' offered many suggested alternatives, e.g., 'We have sinned against you and against our neighbour' rather than 'We have sinned against you and against our fellow men'; 'Bless the Lord all men and women on earth', rather than 'Bless the Lord all men on the earth'; and 'He emptied himself taking the form of a servant: and was born in human likeness', rather than 'He emptied himself taking the form of a servant: and was born in the likeness of men.'[13] However, it took the line of a previous Liturgical Commission and refused to concern itself with matters touching upon the maleness, or otherwise, of God. '[It] does not share the view sometimes heard that male pronouns and possessive adjectives in relation to God are inappropriate, and on *that* issue simply wishes to conform to scriptural and traditional usage.'[14]

Janet Morley's book *All Desires Known* (1988)[15] and another book of feminist prayers, which at least evoked women's distinctive experience were quoted – 'O God, who brought us to birth . . .'.[16] Yet an act of bowdlerization took place which we may think curiously revealing.

In the draft edition of *Making Women Visible* Janet Morley's prayer that begins 'O God our disturber, whose speech is pregnant with power' was changed, without her consent, to 'whose speech is filled with power'. She protested at this alteration and, possibly for this reason, the whole prayer was left out of the final edition. But it appears to be an interesting indication that 'pregnancy' is 'not a nice word' to say in church, with consequent implications about one of the important functions of women.

A very different attitude to inclusive language was shown by the United Reformed Church poet/hymnwriter Brian Wren in his book *What Language Shall I Borrow?* subtitled *God-Talk in Worship: A Male Response to Feminist Theology* (1989).[17] Wren is, at least at the time of writing, almost the only male Christian writer to address the issue of inclusive language at length.

He begins, very promisingly, by seeing inclusive language not as a tiresome invention by feminists but the indication of a much bigger issue. 'I am convinced that male dominance and the construction of "masculinity" are theological problems for *all of us*, whatever our colour, gender, or tradition'.[18] He speaks, he says, as a man, a theologian-poet, and a linguist.

It seems to him that 'every naming of God is a borrowing from human experience'[19] and that language shapes and slants thinking and behaviour. 'To name and depict God almost exclusively in male terms reinforces those distinctions, since it suggests that women are unfit, or less fit than men, to represent the beauty and greatness of God in language.'[20] He speaks of the long struggle to recognize the fact of male dominance in our culture and to understand the theological problems that this poses – the damage that God-talk does if it is couched entirely in male terms. It is damaging to our perception of God and it is damaging to relations between men and women.

Masculinity as we know it – what Wren calls MAWKI for short – is, he suggests, about men remaining in control – of emotion, people, events, nature, etc., and in particular of 'the feminine'. Worse, it is partly defined in terms scornful of femaleness, a scorn which women have picked up and applied themselves. This view of masculinity gives rise to patriarchy, a system based on domination and subordination, in which man (sic) is always 'over' or 'over against'. It is perhaps this that gives rise to the toughness and violence which is such a feature of males in our society. Male sexual potency is equated with force, and gentleness with impotence, a flaw that is tragic enough in personal relations but infinitely worse when it comes to war. Men may express anger, but not tender or 'weak' feelings – sadness, fear, worry, loneliness, etc.

A troubling detail is that we tend to speak as if the male is 'the norm', that all human beings are, or should be, like MAWKI, and that women are a slightly ridiculous other, softhearted, empathetic, weak, helpless. Women have often been shown in plays and films as helpless, unable to protect or defend themselves, and pornography plays upon their weakness and submission. Christianity, while it may theoretically deplore pornography and the degradation of women, subtly promotes it since, while God is depicted virtually always in male terms, 'the other half of humanity, created co-equally in God's image and likeness, is not fit to depict that divine life'.[21]

Like Joseph Campbell, Wren thinks that part of our problem is our inability to understand and profit by metaphor,but it is not only that metaphor is misunderstood, but that we 'see and worship God through the eyes of a flawed maleness' and this 'puts us in danger of worshipping an idol'.[22] Wren gives a name to this idol: KINGAFAP – the King-God-Almighty-Father-Protector. He suggests that this might not be too bad if it represented one set of metaphors among many, some of them feminine, but in true patriarchal style it wants to take over, to assume control. 'God *is* King' it whispers.[23] Brian Wren ends with a great plea not merely for a more comprehensive language, but a changed theology and a different sort of Christian society, exactly what some of his critics fear most.

In 1986 Janet Morley and Hannah Ward brought out *Celebrating Women*, a collection of prayers all written in inclusive language by a number of women, and the book was an instant success, an original publication that broke new ground and was widely used and copied.

In 1988 Janet Morley published *All Desires Known*, a substantial collection of collects, formal prayers, some intended for eucharist, psalms and poems. In these God is rarely addressed in male terms – an exception is 'Christ our brother' – but in many other terms: 'God our security', 'O God our mystery', 'O God for whom we long' etc.

The prayers both emphasize the part women have played in the Christian story, in the way that the conventional prayers of the Church have rarely done, and also specifically address themselves to the feminine in God. In a Eucharistic prayer there is the following passage:

> Therefore, with the woman who gave you birth,
> the women who befriended you and fed you,
> who argued with you and touched you,
> the women who anointed you for death,
> the women who met you, risen from the dead,
> and with all your lovers throughout the ages,
> we praise you, saying:
>
> Holy, holy, holy, etc.

A collect for the feast day of Julian of Norwich says:

> Christ our true mother,
> you have carried us within you,
> laboured with us,
> and brought us forth to bliss . . . [25]

Again and again there are images with a female connotation – carrying in the womb, labouring, feeding, caring for, bringing an extraordinary tenderness and intimacy to the prayers.

These prayers have been very widely used in feminist and other circles in the churches, and some groups have carried on the task Janet Morley began, and started writing their own liturgies and planning their own rituals. One such is the St Hilda Community of East London, a community of women and men, which began in February 1987, partly to hold what they called 'non-sexist' services, and partly to affirm the ministry of women priests by inviting women priests from overseas, and others living in this country, to celebrate for them.

They began by using Janet Morley's prayers, including some that she wrote specially for them, and gradually wrote many of their own, also experimenting with a 'non-hierarchical' form of service. Gradually they have developed a style of shared leadership, of participation of virtually everybody in a service – in readings, discussions, intercessions, in cup and bread passed round, and frequently other 'joining in' activities such as washing one another's hands, and circle dancing. Everyone is expected to learn how to put together a liturgy and this has led both to questions about traditional customs, to new and original ideas, and to a deeper understanding of what does and doesn't make a ritual 'work' for a community.[26]

Such groups give a sense of belonging both to those who feel uncomfortable in traditional forms of church worship yet still attend them, and those who feel unable to take any part in such things. Women, not surprisingly, have taken particular pleasure in them, have, in some cases, really 'found themselves' for the first time in a place where they and their kind were taken seriously and affirmed and where they might play an integral part. Some men, too, have appreciated seeing their own convictions about a different sort of relationship between men and women being carried into action, and have also enjoyed the vitality and freshness of 'inclusive' worship.

There are still some problems about traditional Christian language. Many of us learned to be Christians in the old exclusive language, and there are still hymns and texts that are important to us that would be spoiled by a rigorous application of 'inclusive' ideas. I should hate to see 'God rest ye merry, gentlemen' modernized to some ideologically sound equivalent. We inherit an extraordinarily beautiful language that has been intimately connected with our ancestors' religious beliefs, and even gender considerations do not, in my view, justify heedless modifications in it, with no thought for sound and rhythm. I have sung some fairly appalling up-dates of hymns in recent years, and wonder why more respect is not shown to the writers of them, who did not have the benefit of hindsight about feminist issues. A blanket application of political principles of feminism is no more appropriate here than is any political interference with poetry, literature and art in any other circumstances.

Yet, as Janet Morley and others have demonstrated, it is perfectly possible to add to our vocabulary, our stock of images and our metaphors for God, without destroying what has gone before, indeed by enriching it with good, twentieth-century prayers. It is possible too to make certain alterations to conventional liturgies that are not destructive or aesthetically ludicrous, and which in some cases are an improvement on the original.

There *is*, of course, an important political principle involved, which is why we are suspicious of those who condemn inclusive language root and branch. Those who cannot stomach the idea of a female metaphor being used for God, although a male one does not offend them, are revealing their rejection of the female with a consequent rejection of actual women. This is what we have come to understand in the past ten years, and having understood it we cannot ignore it.

Notes

1. Janet Morley and Hannah Ward, *Celebrating Women*. WIT/MOW 1986.
2. Janet Morley, 'The Faltering Words of Men', in Monica Furlong, ed., *Feminine in the Church* (SPCK 1984), p. 60.
3. Graham Leonard, Iain MacKenzie, Peter Toon, *Let God be God*. Darton, Longman and Todd 1989.
4. *The Alternative Service Book 1980*.
5. Report in *The Church Times*, 26 June 1990.
6. William Oddie, *What Will Happen to God?* SPCK 1984.
7. Joseph Campbell, *The Power of Myth* (Doubleday 1989), p. 56.
8. Liturgical Commission of the General Synod of the Church of England, *Making Women Visible; Inclusive Language for Use with the Alternative Service Book* (Church House Publishing 1989), p. 19, para. 71.
9. Mary Daly, *Beyond God the Father*. Boston: Beacon Press 1973; Women's Press 1986.
10. Janet Morley, 'The Faltering Words of Men', pp. 64 – 5.
11. United Church of Canada, *Bad Language in Church*. 1983.
12. *Making Women Visible*, p. 2, para. 5.
13. *Making Women Visible*, pp. 28 – 9.
14. *Making Women Visible*, p. 2, para. 8.
15. Janet Morley, *All Desires Known*. WIT/MOW 1988.
16. *Making Women Visible*, p. 28.
17. Brian Wren, *What Language Shall I Borrow?* SCM Press 1989.
18. Wren, p. ix.

19. Wren, p. 1.
20. Wren, p. 3.
21. Wren, p. 55.
22. Wren, p. 123.
23. Wren, p. 125.
24. Morley, *All Desires Known*, p. 42.
25. Morley, *All Desires Known*, p. 25.
26. The St Hilda Community, *Women Included*. SPCK 1991.

5 · 'Mañana, Lord, Mañana' – The Great Women's Ordination Debate

THE DOCTRINE OF THE UNRIPE TIME

Because
Women have been silent in the Church
for two thousand years, but when they
speak they are told they are strident

Because
Women have been invisible in the
Church for centuries, but when they
want to be seen they are told they are
status seekers.

Because
Women are told that they cannot
represent Christ, though they are also
told that suffering is their lot

Because
Women are told that they are too
fragile to be priests, and they had
better get back to caring for children,
the sick, the senile, the crazy, and the
terminally ill.

Because
Women are accused of splitting the
Church when others threaten to leave it

Because
While everything else has its kairos,
for women the time never seems to be
ripe.

For these, and other reasons, I am a member of MOW.

How about you?

Advertisement in *Chrysalis*, the
magazine of the Movement for the Ordination of Women.

Priesthood should be free of worldly distinctions. It is rather like that most
splendid of the Articles of the Church of England which declares that the
unworthiness of ministers does not invalidate the sacraments. If unworthi-
ness in men does not, the divine distribution of sexual attributes certainly
should not.

Edward Norman, *The Times*, 24 February 1987

ON THE ISSUE of women priests the Church of England has behaved rather like St Augustine in the matter of chastity. 'Give us women priests, Lord, but not yet.' A *Chrysalis* cartoon had Dr Runcie gazing heavenwards with the heartfelt prayer 'Mañana, Lord, mañana!'

The issue of making women priests has a sort of scandal of particularity about it. If women have not been priests for two thousand years of Christian history, why now? Why them?

Did women always secretly wonder what sort of job they would have made of being priests? Certainly many medieval abbesses exercised functions very like that of a bishop, and it seems likely that in the earliest centuries of the Church, some of the women St Paul mentions as opening their homes to Christian communities may have blessed bread and wine (in the tradition of the Jewish wife and mother), or acted as deacon. Many throughout have had gifts which would have made them admirable priests, but it is difficult to wonder aloud about opportunities from which you are debarred, by education as well as by gender – it takes a very strong independence of mind, or an overwhelming sense of vocation. But women in other walks of life have sometimes had both those things and yet had their gifts suppressed, like Mendelssohn's gifted sister Fanny who, in order to get her work played at all, had to pretend Felix had composed it. Only when Queen Victoria particularly admired Fanny's composition could Felix keep quiet no longer, feeling obliged to acknowledge his sister's skill. But few people have ever heard of Fanny Mendelssohn.

Maude Royden, 1876–1956, was both gifted and confident. She was the youngest child of a rich shipowner in Liverpool and enjoyed a confidence born of wealth. She attended Cheltenham Ladies' College – a school she picked for herself – and Lady Margaret Hall, Oxford. Her education completed, she found herself, like so many well-to-do girls of her generation, 'helping at home'. This gradually yielded to charitable work in a depressing slum in Liverpool – the Victoria Women's Settlement – and she went to help in a country parish where her friend Hudson Shaw was Rector. It was there that as a university extension lecturer she discovered that she had rare gifts as a speaker, and as time went on she began to use her talent more and more, to speak in favour of women's suffrage, and about peace issues.

When Hudson Shaw became Rector of St Botolph's, Bishopsgate, he asked her to do what women were never invited to do – to read the lesson, which she did with her usual clear delivery, although, she said later 'with trembling lips'. No protest followed, and perhaps emboldened by this Shaw asked her if she would give some addresses in the church. In September 1918 Maude Royden gave an address at a lunch-time service held on a week-day, speaking, as she was well qualified to do, about the League of Nations and Christianity. The church was packed to the galleries. This event brought a gentle rebuke from the Bishop of London, requesting Shaw not to invite another woman for a week-day service without consulting him, and forbidding him to include one in a Sunday service.

Bishop Winnington-Ingram claimed to support women's suffrage, but when Convocation discussed women preaching in February 1919, the bishop, after praising women's gifts and acknowledging their frustration, would not support a motion that women be allowed to speak in consecrated buildings, but proposed setting up a committee to discuss the subject. Irritated at this obvious delaying tactic, Shaw invited Maude Roydon to give the Three Hours Service in St Botolph's on Good Friday, and she accepted. By Maundy Thursday the Bishop had forbidden Shaw to hold this service in his church, so it was held in a packed Parish Room with a large audience listening through the windows.

This incident, which aroused enormous interest in the Press, could perhaps be said to have started the modern women's movement in the Church of England. Women were already incensed by an incident during the National Mission of 1917 when women up and down the country undertook to carry and read in church a special message from their bishops. In London scandalized gentlemen protested to the Bishop of London and as a result, Bishop Winnington-Ingram declared that women might only read aloud in church to congregations of women and children, and then not from the lectern or the pulpit. 'They were apparently to speak from soap boxes or from a perch on the reredos', said the young Rebecca West sarcastically.[1]

Maude Royden's Good Friday address stirred up a controversy already present as a strand in the suffragette debate about whether women might be ordained, and this uncovered an extraordinary fantasy of a High Churchman, Athelstan Riley, that women were preparing a plot to 'attack' the Church. Rage and ridicule followed any suggestion that women might offer themselves for priesthood. 'For any sane person' said the *Church Times* 'the thing is so grotesque that he must refuse to discuss it. . . . The monstrous regiment of women in politics would be bad enough but a monstrous regiment of priestesses would be a thousandfold worse. . . . [We] are not inclined to treat [it] as a sane scheme . . . .'[2]

Athelstan Riley came up with the 'clincher' so often applied in such debates. '(Women) will not stoop to copy the Mother of God, who by her obedience and her humility co-operated with her Maker in His scheme for the salvation of mankind, and who by her earthly self-effacement has set an example to all women . . . .'[3]

Maude Royden eventually became disheartened at her attempts to work within the Church of England, and when offered a job as preacher at the big Nonconformist chapel, the City Temple, she accepted it. She died hurt and embittered that her own church valued her so little.

Maude had lived in a period in which she and her contemporaries questioned all the accepted ideas about 'woman's place'. In 1909 the Reverend Claude Hinscliff had started the Church League for Women's Suffrage, with the admirable help of Edward Hicks, Bishop of Lincoln, a man who deplored the *waste* of women, whom he described as 'the unenfranchised, the unrepresented, the unemployed, the unprivileged'. Though primarily concerned with getting women the vote by non-militant means, it also sought to draw out what Hinscliff called 'the deep religious significance of the women's movement'.[4] By 1914 it had over 5000 members, both men and women. By 1930, with the vote secured, the League became torn by disagreements between those who wanted to press for women's ordination, and those whose concern was 'the depreciation of women's work and total ignoring of their status in the Church'.[5] Two groups came out of this, The Anglican Group for the Ordination of Women, and the Society for the Equal Ministry of Men and Women in the Church (changed again in 1957 to Society for the Ministry of Women in the Church). Maude Royden became the President.

The Archbishops' Commission on the Ministry of Women of 1920 did its best to squelch discussion on women's ordination informing the world that 'the restriction of the ministry of the priesthood to men originated in a generation which was guided by the special gifts of the Holy Spirit.'[6] Argue with that, if you dare. The Lambeth Conference of 1920 came out firmly against women's ordination.

The Lambeth Conference of 1930 took the same line. A memorandum on *Women and the Priesthood* prepared by the Society was sent to the Archbishop of Canterbury as a contribution to the discussion. Another group compiled letters for women who felt called to the priesthood. One described 'the ardent and overpowering longing, when preparing the altar for Celebrations, to be a man, just to be able to celebrate the Divine Mysteries'.

Conference was not moved by these communications. Once again it reiterated the total impossibility of women's ordination. It discussed the possibility of deaconesses assisting at Holy Communion, and participation in churching and burial offices. The idea was dismissed.

There was still enough vitality left from the suffrage debates, and the new thinking about women, for the Church of England to feel obliged to make some more adequate explanation of its thinking. Once again the Archbishops' Commission sat, and once again in 1935 it reported negatively. 'We believe that it would be impossible for the male members of the average Anglican congregation to be present at a service at which a woman ministered without becoming unduly conscious of her sex.'[7] The potential women priests are so attractive – every last woman of them it would seem – that the mere sight of them is guaranteed to arouse wild passions of lust in a male congregation. Going to church was never like this.

Luckily for a hierarchy clearly at its wits' end, some of the impetus for the first great wave of the women's movement was dying down. 'Whereas the first three decades of the century saw considerable expansion and development in the scope of women's work for the Church,' says Brian Heeney, 'the movement stalled in the early 1930s, to regain momentum only with the renewal of militant feminism and the vigorous (but unsuccessful) drive for female ordination in the 1970s.'[8]

Between the first wave and the second, however, one very important event occurred – the ordination of a Chinese deaconess, Li Tim Oi, by Bishop R. O. Hall of Hong Kong and South China in 1944. Struggling to maintain a Christian presence in a diocese torn by war and invasion the bishop was desperately short of priests. He summoned Li Tim Oi, who made a long, dangerous journey through the Japanese lines, met the bishop in Macao, and was ordained priest by him.

This guaranteed that women's ordination was once again on the agenda at the next Lambeth Conference, in 1948. There, according to a later bishop of Taiwan, James Pong, 'opposition was so vehement that Bishop Hall and the Rev Miss Lee both submitted to the pressures of the then prevailing opinion for the sake of the harmony of the church.'[9] Mainly from loyalty to Hall, Li Tim Oi withdrew from working as a priest, though she did not resign her orders.

When I became an Anglican in 1948 I remember asking a few timid questions about why women could not become priests. The standard answer at the time, like so many standard answers, was taken from C. S. Lewis:

> Suppose the reformer stops saying that a good woman may be like God and begins saying God is like a good woman. Suppose he says that we might just as well pray to 'Our Mother which art in Heaven' as to 'Our Father'. Suppose he suggests that the

Incarnation might just as well have taken a female as a male form, and the Second Person of the Trinity be as well called the Daughter as the Son. . . . Now it is surely the case that if all these supposals were ever carried into effect we should be embarked on a different religion. Goddesses have, of course, been worshipped: many religions have had priestesses. But they are religions quite different in character from Christianity.[10]

Yet there must have been some sense of ruffled female feathers needing to be smoothed because in the Lambeth Conference of 1958 speakers made an almost unprecedented point of actually congratulating women on their labours in the Church. There was a recommendation – a slightly odd one, we may think – that women should be used 'where pioneer work has to be done'. The 1968 Lambeth Conference, like some huge dinosaur dimly aware that the environment about it was changing in unfriendly ways, admitted that the arguments for and against the ordination of women were 'inconclusive' and asked national and regional churches to study the matter and report their findings.

It was too late for that sort of delaying tactic, however. The little animals were already taking over, and in 1971 the Anglican Consultative Council (the most senior advisory body in the Anglican Communion), chaired by the then Archbishop of Canterbury, Dr Ramsey, passed 'Resolution 28' which, among other clauses, advised the Bishop of Hong Kong, Gilbert Baker, and any other bishop in a like frame of mind, that with the approval of his own province, he might ordain women to the priesthood. Baker at once ordained two women, Joyce Bennett and Jane Hwang, and Li Tim Oi was restored to the status of a priest. 'As we try to cope with the needs of a huge population – in which half the industrial workers are women – ' Baker declared, 'I believe we are impelled by the Holy Spirit to make better provisions for the needs of men and women alike through a ministry more representative of humanity as a whole.'

These new developments threw the Episcopal Church of the USA into a ferment. A large group of women there had already been undergoing theological training in the hope of entering the priesthood; the Civil Rights movement of the sixties, in which a number of them had taken part, had fired them both with a sense of justice and of the possibility of change. Some of them went to discuss the matter with the Presiding Bishop, James Allin. They found his manner towards them offensive – implying that he liked women 'to be women', addressing them as 'girls', and when one of their number got up to 'go to the bathroom' telling her sharply to sit down. The oldest member of the party, Jeanette Piccard, spoke up: 'Boy, I'm old enough to be your grandmother, and nobody calls me "girl".'

General Convention discussed the matter and ended with a split vote – the House of Bishops in favour, the House of Deputies against. Three bishops – Daniel Corrigan, Robert de Witt, and Edward Welles – declared themselves ready to ordain women without waiting. On 29 July 1974, eleven women, later known as 'the Philadelphia Eleven', were 'irregularly' ordained priest in the Church of the Advocate, Philadelphia. They were Marrill Bittner, Alla Bozarth-Campbell, Alison Cheek, Emily Hewitt, Carter Heyward, Suzanne Hiatt, Marie Moorfield, Jeanette Piccard, Betty Bone Schiess, Katrina Swanson and Nancy Wittig. The crucifer was a young woman called Barbara Harris.

Not surprisingly a huge row broke out in the Episcopal Church, with bishops threatening legal action, and all the women feeling that it was unlikely they would ever be accepted as priests. In 1976, however, General Convention voted again, agreeing both to ordain women and to accept the ministry of the eleven women.

Women in other parts of the Anglican Church had watched this development with fascination. Canada and New Zealand were quick to follow suit and started ordaining women priests in 1975 and 1976.

Meanwhile the Houses of Parliament had passed the Sex Discrimination Act in 1975. Section 19 (1) of the Act states that 'it does not apply to employment for purposes of an organized religion where the employment is limited to one sex so as to comply with the doctrines of the religion or avoid offending the religious susceptibilities of a significant number of its followers.'

The dilemma of those who wanted to see the Bill become law was a difficult one. If the situation of women in the churches was included in it then strong vested interests in both the House of Commons and the House of Lords would oppose it, with consequent damage to women in other situations. A group called the Dorcas Group from New Malden asked the Home Secretary why the churches should be excluded from the provisions of the Act, and received the reply that including women would infringe 'religious freedom'. But Members of both Houses had consulted with the Anglican Group for the Ordination of Women who had counselled exclusion, not alas, on the grounds that this might damage women in general, but that 'we did not want to win our case by means of court of law battles, as the Church in Sweden had done resulting in much bitterness.'

The Church of England began to move at a snail's pace towards women's ordination, though General Synod in 1975, not quite indifferent to the spirit of the times, voted that 'there was no fundamental objection to the ordination of women to the priesthood', a development that gave great heart to many.

Yet there was, of course, considerable opposition to the idea. The early letters to the *Church Times, The Times* and other newspapers on the subject often imply that the idea, though repulsive, was so remote as scarcely to be worth taking seriously. Women are reminded of their fragility, of their emotional vulnerability, of their duties as mothers, of how crass it is of them to think of 'rights' and 'status' in connection with the priesthood, of their refusal to be obedient and submissive as Mary was obedient and submissive.

At this early stage of the debate, however, perhaps only the Church Union, and the Bishop of Truro (Graham Leonard) anticipated the true nature of the struggle that lay ahead.

The women themselves were little better organized than the opposition. The events in Hong Kong, in Canada, New Zealand, and above all, in the USA, gave a feeling that things were gradually moving in their direction. Such organization as existed – the Society for the Ministry of Women in the Church, and the Anglican Group for the Ordination of Women – had been in existence for a long time, and had grown used to living without high expectation of change.

Suddenly, however, change came through the determination of Deaconess Una Kroll, a woman of remarkable energy, courage and spiritual depth, who was to inspire many who till then had taken little interest in the debate. (In Scotland a similar role was being played by Daphne Hampson.) Una Kroll brought a new emphasis to the debate by beginning to talk of women and men *sharing* together, of having a complementary ministry within the Church, a ministry which would offer a telling critique of a world outside where too often women were marginalized, ignored, put down and abused. Back in the 1960s she had rejected the separate, and rather ladylike, training offered to deaconesses, and had applied and been accepted by the Southwark Ordination Course (a part-time course which she attended alongside her work as a GP), where she studied on equal terms alongside the men. Like so many women since, she watched her male contemporaries go on to the priesthood after a year of being a deacon, unable to join them.

Capable and intelligent, with the confidence of a successful professional woman, Una Kroll revealed in her own person the wastefulness of the Church of England in debarring women like her from the priesthood. She was also, partly through her work as a doctor in a poor part of London, aware of the many hardships, lost opportunities, and miseries of women in our society, and saw a link between a church which did not ordain women, and a church which did not care very much about women at all, or which preached that suffering was women's natural lot.

Unlike most deaconesses she was open about her resentment, discussing it with the Press, on radio programmes, in public debates. The world of the media was new to the whole issue of women priests, and initially fairly hostile, although Una Kroll was a brilliant broadcaster. She organized public meetings, held many private meetings with influential church men and, with Deaconess Elsie Baker, then working at the Church of the Ascension, Blackheath, set up an organization to further her aims of complementarity between women and men – Christian Parity.

Una Kroll's outspoken criticism of the Church, at that time new and shocking, produced resentment, and the first charges (later to be become so wearisomely familiar whenever a female voice was raised in question or criticism), of stridency and aggression.

As articulate women began to gather, to admit to suppressed vocations to the priesthood, to enter the theological colleges, to hold their first liturgies which gave space to 'the feminine', to argue with their vicars and fellow-Christians about the invisible role women had been forced to play, there was a mood of hope. The Synod motion of 1975, the developments in the USA and in other countries, suggested a 'wind of change', and since Britain had so many women of excellent quality it seemed as if in a year or two the necessary legislation would be passed.

In this mood of hope women went to the General Synod of November, 1978. The motion to be debated that day was 'That this Synod asks the Standing Committee to prepare and bring forward legislation to remove the barriers to the ordination of women to the priesthood and their consecration to the episcopate.' The House debated it for six and a half hours before a packed public gallery, and then voted, registering 521 votes, the largest number Synod had ever recorded on any subject. The House of Bishops had thirty-two votes in favour, seventeen against, the House of Laity one hundred and twenty in favour and one hundred and six against, the House of Clergy ninety-four in favour and one hundred and forty-nine against. There was, therefore, an overall majority of twenty-six, but since the Motion was Article 8 business, only a majority of two thirds could pass it, and the Motion fell.

Una Kroll, who had toiled harder than anyone to bring about a favourable vote, let out a memorable cry from the public gallery – needless to say, an intervention which was later treated as a dreadful scandal. 'We asked you for bread and you gave us a stone' she cried, and that sense of outrage has echoed all down the years since, as women have pointed out their exclusion, very often to deaf or unsympathetic ears. Margaret Duggan, reporting the day in the *Church Times*, describing herself as 'a reluctant convert to women's ordination' nevertheless said she had been 'ashamed and disgusted' at that day's work, in particular at the sense of the 'Catholic group' following carefully laid plans to defeat the Motion. 'The proponents' she said 'were just not geared to face the highly organized opposition.'

The women who had worked for ordination felt shocked, betrayed, humiliated. I was away in America during this debate, and well remember the spate of letters I received describing the occasion. Some of my correspondents vowed to leave the Church (and some did), others were in despair and anger.

Painful as all this was, the outcome was significant. For the first, though not the last time, on this issue, rebuff evoked anger, and produced energy for change. Within a week of Synod (while the women's opponents were gleefully boasting in the *Church Times* that the issue had been defeated 'for the foreseeable future'), there began to be talk of a 'national movement' to put the women's case. A number of leading women met at the house of Mrs Diana Collins in Amen Court, St Paul's, to discuss the possibility. Just before the Synod Mrs Collins and the Earl of March had organized a declaration in favour of women's ordination and asked leading members of the Church of England, the community, the professions, the arts, sciences, and the business world to sign. Some 230 had done so – peers, judges, actors, diplomats, politicians. It was an issue which cut right across political barriers, and even across barriers of churchmanship, though this did not immediately become evident.

In July of 1979 distinguished signatories and those who had played a leading part in working for women's ordination met at the Church Commissioners' Building on Millbank, and approved a constitution drawn up by a working group to bring into existence the Movement for the Ordination of Women. A bishop, Stanley Booth-Clibborn, Bishop of Manchester, was invited to be Moderator, the chairperson of MOW. It was felt at the time that this might be a necessary way to secure respectability, and an entrée to episcopal thinking, but in 1982, partly at the bishop's instigation, it was thought more appropriate to have a woman as Moderator – the first of these was Monica Furlong. There were two women Vice-Moderators, Christian Howard and Jo Garcia. (Later, when women occupied the Moderatorship, a bishop was asked to be Vice-Moderator, a practice given up in 1988, when this no longer seemed particularly appropriate.)

Those who knew most about church organizations prophesied that the numbers would rise to about twelve hundred and stop there. It rose to four thousand, five thousand, and now stands at almost six thousand. It began modestly with the Executive Secretary, Mrs Margaret Webster, occupying a spare desk in the office of Christian Action. Within a year, because of the kindness of the Vicar of St Stephen's, Rochester Row, it had its own excellent offices at Napier Hall in Hide Place, which became the permanent headquarters from which to work and plan.

At first there was the tentative phase of a new organization seeking a style. Because it took into itself members from all the existing organizations pushing for a new role for women in the Church, it had both a radical and conservative constituency to attend to, and these groups, together with the more middle-of-the-road members, had to set themselves the task of learning to get along with new bedfellows. There was perhaps a basic conflict that was almost impossible to address – many supporters were very respectable people, yet the legislation had radical implications that perhaps nobody at that time had fully perceived. There was also the question of what sort of action should be taken to draw public and ecclesiastical attention to women's situation. Radicals were in favour of vigorous demonstrations of one kind and another, conservatives feared that this would be 'counter-productive', a word that was to be heard many, many times, in endless discussions. None was very extreme – in retrospect, the shyness and timidity is striking. It took a lot of courage for women who had been bred to be quiet, polite and obedient, to confront their fathers in God. The most frightening aspect of it was discovering how angry we were – it felt disturbing and 'unchristian'. Only as time went on did we learn the energy-potential of anger, and begin to speak with more confident voices, and in stronger terms.

The first startling event in which MOW members were involved took place on 1 July 1980. It was Petertide, and an ordination was taking place in St Paul's, with a congregation of thousands, and some MOW members asked the then Bishop of London, Gerald Ellison, if he would say a prayer in the course of the service for women who would like to be ordained but could not be. The Bishop was, in fact, a supporter of women's ordination in the general way that so many liberal-minded bishops were and are, but he refused this simple request, saying that this would 'spoil the day for the young men', and that it would only be justified if the opposition were allowed to put an alternative point of view. (To the women, of course, it seemed as if the whole occasion represented 'the alternative point of view'.)

A group of eight, women and men, attended the service. When the ordination proper was over, and the creed was being sung, they unfurled banners saying 'Ordain Women' in front of each section of the congregation. All were hustled out, one of the male demonstrators actually being struck by one of the wandsmen (sidesmen), although no resistance had been shown, nor voice raised.

It was, of course, a three-day wonder, with coverage on television and radio, an article by one of the demonstrators in *The Times* the next day, and full coverage in the *Church Times* at the end of the week. Predictably, many people were 'disgusted'.

One who was not was the new Archbishop of Canterbury, Dr Runcie, who invited the leader of the demonstrators to visit him at Lambeth and discuss the matter. She took with her a representative group of women, including two Deaconesses, one of whom broke down in tears as she described her intense disappointment at never realizing her lifelong sense of vocation to be a priest, and her realization that now she was too old. Dr Runcie was kindness itself, listening carefully to all that the women had to tell him and promising to remember it. Yet he wondered that they were prepared to set the Church on the thorny path of wrestling with the issue – it seemed to puzzle him that they wished to do that – and he repeated, as he was to do on many more occasions, his belief that 'the time was not ripe'.

The St Paul's demonstration started a spate of rather less disruptive activities at ordinations up and down the country – groups of women standing outside cathedrals and giving out flowers or leaflets to worshippers, women kneeling or standing through the service, sometimes wearing a sash to indicate the purpose of their protest. The proponents were not alone in such demonstrations, however.

At Llandaff Cathedral in 1981, when the Church of Wales ordained a woman, Iris Thomas, as deacon (the tenth they had so ordained, in sharp distinction to the Church of England who made women deaconesses) there was a demonstration in protest. Francis Bown, of Ecclesia, sent the inevitable letter to the *Church Times*. 'The attempted ordination of women to the diaconate' (he would not accept that such an ordination was possible) 'is therefore the thin end of a very thick wedge and represents the first step on the road that leads to the total abandonment of any claim to possess Catholic Faith and Order.'

MOW began what was to be a successful publishing programme by producing a Study Pack, and various occasional papers by clergy, theologians and others that had bearing on the ordination issue. Approaches were made to Trusts to obtain funds.

In March 1981 an appointment was made by the Prime Minister that was to have far-reaching effects on the youthful movement to get women ordained. The appointment caused a good deal of resentment, mainly because Mrs Thatcher took the unusual, though permissible, step of choosing the second rather than the first name on the list of two candidates submitted to her by the Church of England. Newspapers reported her as doing this as a reaction to 'a move to the Left wing of politics by some leading figures of the Church of England'. There was so much protest about her decision that her office were obliged to publish a statement, saying the 'procedures had been meticulously followed'.

Graham Leonard, Bishop of Truro, already known as a hardline opponent of women priests, became Bishop of London. 'Dr Leonard', said the *Sunday Telegraph*, 'believes that there are different roles in society. One of those for a woman was bringing up children and running a home. Jobs could not be played with or interchanged.'

In contrast Dr Runcie himself seemed almost warmly feminist, stating in an interview in *Woman's Realm*, 'If priesthood is to represent God to mankind and mankind to God in days when exclusive male leadership is no longer the case in most walks of life, it's hard to justify the fact that men alone can represent God to mankind and mankind to God. I therefore now think that the best arguments are in favour of opening the priesthood to women . . . I've pointed out more than once that in Church circles women are regarded as pew fodder rather than leaders.'

However he went on: 'I think unity among Christians is more important than the ordination of women.' Asked if women had not pressed their claims of recognition hard enough in the churches he said that

> women have been through history, the passive people in the life of the Church – as seen in the tranquility of Mary, the motherhood of Mary, the suffering of Mary. These are the ways in which the best of femininity is focused in tradition and in which women are not seen as 'pushy' at all. That's why some of us need quite a time to get used to the stridency of some modern women's rights campaigners.'

It is impossible to quarrel with the statement that historically women have been passive in the Church, but it is noticeable that he is not pointing out that they have had no choice, and that it is from the frustration and invisibility of a forced 'passivity' that women now make their claims strongly. One feels his nostalgia for 'the best of femininity' and the shrinking from what is seen as 'stridency' with very little real grasp of what the women actually feel or are trying to say.

Well might he have nostalgic dreams of passive femininity. In April 1981 two vicars' wives, Susan Dowell and Linda

Hurcombe, published a book *Dispossessed Daughters of Eve*,[11] which pitched into the Church with a shout of indignation and a honed feminism rarely seen until then. It claimed that the Church of England was 'male-obsessed' from its choirs to its theology, from its clergy to its language. It mercilessly attacked the sentimentality of Mariolatry, pointing out how little those clergy who loved Mary most showed concern for actual flesh-and-blood women, or for anything feminine apart from their reverential attitude to motherhood. The book went on, perhaps a little randomly, to fling accusations at a dozen Aunt Sallies, hitting some of them, missing others, but exuding a cheerful energy and lack of respect which was received by many women as a welcome tonic. The tone of voice of the debate was beginning to change with women becoming less timid, less fearful of being thought a nuisance. Dowell and Hurcombe turned being a nuisance into a minor art form.

Just how different were the outlooks of women and many church men became evident that summer when the World Council of Churches met in Sheffield to discuss 'the Community of Women and Men in the Church'. The subject was topical and attracted a large audience from churches all over the world. The Archbishop of Canterbury was one of the principal speakers and spoke with care, intelligence, and a clear wish to enter the debate helpfully. He began by saying that he hoped to avoid what Rosemary Ruether had called 'a high-minded neutrality which hides a commitment to the *status quo*'. He admitted that, in the Anglican tradition at least, the church's ministry *to* women had often been 'exercised badly and insensitively'. He also showed how all churches in the Protestant tradition had taken quite legitimate areas of ministry *from* women, and failed to see that they had any role beyond sexuality and child-rearing. As a result of this 'ministry has become a masculine professional status occupation'.

Yet, he went on to say, women did minister – as teachers, contemplative nuns, counsellors, spiritual advisers. So far, so good, but then he added, 'There is a real danger that an over-concentration on the issues involved in the ordination of women may reinforce a clericalist view of the church: the only ministry worth exercising is an *ordained* one.' This is a point of view that women in and out of the Movement for the Ordination of Women have uttered to one another often enough, sometimes in negative criticism of women who already work within the church structures, yet to have it said in the context of a keynote speech with such major exposure, when feelings were still raw from the rebuff of 1978, gave it a very different flavour. What it seemed to be saying was that there was no need to bother about ordination when there were so many other opportunities open to women, and what was read into it, correctly, was that the Archbishop, while well-meaning towards women, did not want to move at the moment. He went on, predictably, to speak of 'patience', and then moved to a rather crude impression of the women's movement. 'It divides between those who want to burn their bras, refuse to marry, and insist on doing all that men do – even to playing games which are anatomically painful – and those who ask for something more difficult to articulate. That something is the freedom of women.'

His interpretation of this was extraordinary, and probably more revealing of his attitude to women than he intended.

> Freedom . . . consists in *not* being constrained by male attitudes to ministry, to work, to the family, or above all to God. But to be heard in the very depths of their being: in their love which has to extend to troublesome children and in that extension learns to reach out beyond conventional boundaries and which has often to accept a measure of physical weakness. This may breed not militancy but a very real humility. It takes many forms: women need and have to accept their need – for maternity leave, for retraining, for care facilities sometimes for their children – but above all they need to accept from others an understanding. . . .

It is difficult to read this now, as many found it difficult to listen to it even then, without being astonished at the unconscious sexism, at the age-old suggestion that women must be humble, grateful, weak, and tied to their children. (Don't men need 'care facilities' sometimes for *their* children, not to mention some recognition of *their* own needs and weakness?) Women have rarely seen themselves as weak, knowing well the physical and psychological strength it takes to survive as a woman. To the Archbishop's surprise (as he later freely admitted) many of his world audience, further on in their own thinking about women and sexism, found his well-meant speech wholly unacceptable.

In November 1981, ten years after the decision of the Anglican Consultative Council and the ordination of Joyce Bennett and Jane Hwang in Hong Kong, General Synod decided to approve the admission of women to the diaconate – that is to admit them to 'holy Orders', the first stage of which is to become a deacon: a different thing from being a deaconess and not in Orders at all. It is difficult not to see this as a sop thrown to the women in recognition that they were not going to pipe down until *something* had been given to them. It was also difficult not to be suspicious of a sudden enthusiasm, to be repeated at later Synods, for what is called a 'permanent diaconate', that is to say a state where deacons do not go on to become priests. It seemed a coincidence that it was only as the admission of women to the diaconate was under discussion that this suddenly seemed such an appealing idea.

At this appropriate time a National Opinion Poll showed that 75% of the population thought that women should be eligible for the priesthood, and of those who claimed membership of the Church of England 81% were in favour.

While the issue continued to be debated in Synod, an Englishwoman, Elizabeth Canham, had gone to the United States, completed her training for the priesthood there, and was now ordained in the cathedral of Newark, New Jersey. She expressed a hope that in the not too distant future she might be able to return home and use her ministry there.

In the meanwhile she made a fleeting visit, and in January 1982 celebrated the Eucharist privately with a group of women previously invited in the St Paul's Deanery. (Thanks to the very generous hospitality of Margaret and Alan Webster – the Dean – the Deanery was to play an important part as a gathering place for women engaged on the ordination issue. Meetings, parties, meals, many of them run or attended by one, or both, of the Websters, were where many feelings found expression, ideas were formulated, and disagreements were survived.) In fact, by this stage of MOW's life, many Eucharists had been held in private homes when American women priests were visiting – Alison Palmer, Suzanne Hiatt and Bliss Williams Brown all come to mind. These were all conducted without publicity, but a New Zealand woman priest, Janet Crawford, had celebrated fairly publicly at the MOW Conference in the previous year. The Bishop of Derby, Cyril Bowles, was present, and raised no objection.

The Deanery Eucharist was, however, advertised in the *Church Times*, and the Bishop of London at once reacted sharply, drawing the Archbishop of Canterbury's attention to what, he said, was an 'illegal' action. The Dean, however, said that he had not thought that a service performed in one's own home was under the jurisdiction of ecclesiastical discipline.

Considering the various aspects of women's ordination – in particular the plea of Cardinal Hume, some ten years previously, for time – Clifford Longley of *The Times* predicted that 'the Church is going to be more and more embarrassed by feminist dissent as the months go by.' The Church of England, he suggested, had 'done the right thing' by the world Christian communion in not rushing ahead to ordain women, but was now gaining the 'reputation as an institution which has not the courage to make hard choices'.

In July 1983, Deaconess Ann Hoad led a silent walk-out of thirteen deaconesses from an ordination service in Southwark Cathedral. The women held a 'wilderness' liturgy in the street outside, eating honey cake and drinking milk – a sort of Exodus meal. They were supported by some sixty women and men who had come there to join in their witness.

There was a very different sort of witness in January 1984 when MOW decided to celebrate the forty years Li Tim Oi had spent as a priest in the Anglican Communion, and held a special service for her in Westminster Abbey. Gilbert Baker, who had succeeded R.O. Hall as Bishop of Hong

Kong, presided, Joyce Bennett preached, and the Abbey was packed, with nineteen bishops attending, and many women priests from abroad. The service was deeply moving and many wept in the course of it. At lunch after the service a presentation was made to Li Tim Oi, at which she made a humorous speech in moving, broken English. 'It has taken forty years and women here still cannot be ordained. In the Church everything takes a long, long time. . . .' *Ecclesia* (subtitle 'fellowship of concerned Anglicans') printed an advertisement in the *Church Times* the next week complaining that the Abbey had been used for 'little more than a political demonstration'.

MOW members, in collaboration with SPCK, published a collection of papers and essays about the issue of ordaining women, and women's status in general, in a book called *Feminine in the Church* in 1984. At the same time William Oddie published a book called *What will happen to God?* in which, by citing extreme American feminists such as Mary Daly, he managed to imply that it was the intention of women in the Church of England to destroy it.

A National Opinion Poll conducted in October 1984 showed that 79% of the general population were in favour of women priests, with the figure rising to 84% of those who claimed to be members of the Church of England.

Seven hundred priests and bishops signed an open letter to the Archbishops of Canterbury and York urging them to give a lead in the matter of the ordination of women. (This body later became known as Priests for Women's Ordination.) Meanwhile the staff and pupils of Westcott House theological college signed a letter urging General Synod to pass the legislation which would allow women to become deacons.

In November 1984, in the first vote on the women's ordination issue since 1978, General Synod began the legal process with a speech in favour of the motion by Ronald Bowlby, Bishop of Southwark. The Archbishop of Canterbury spoke and voted against the motion, the Archbishop of York spoke and voted in favour. Watched by a crowded gallery, Synod carried the motion by 307 votes to 183,

although the *Church Times* and several newspapers had suggested it stood no chance.

In July 1985 Synod voted that women should be allowed
to become deacons, an important first step towards the
priesthood. Most of the 350 deaconesses in the Church were
thought to want the change of status. The Reverend Francis
Bown said that it was 'a grievous blow for all those who
value the Catholic heritage of the Church of England' and
went on to imply that it was 'the beginning of the end
for the Church of England'. The Reverend Peter Geldard,
secretary of the Church Union, warned that it 'would raise
the expectations that women would become priests'.

The Archbishop of York, on the other hand, said that if
one was concerned to reflect the church of the New Testament, then we *should* have women deacons, as they almost
certainly did. Some other opponents of women's ordination
to the priesthood seemed to welcome the idea of ordaining
them as deacons, apparently in the hope that that would
satisfy them, that the Church having gone one mile might
not have to go twain. The decision to ordain women as
deacons was to be enthusiastically and overwhelmingly rati-
fied by Parliament in 1987.

In August the opponents of women's ordination held a
Press Conference at which they launched a new campaign
with an organization called the Association for an Apostolic
Ministry, with the purpose of rivalling MOW in publishing
literature about the women's ordination issue. The Bishop
of Edmonton, Brian Masters, and Dr Margaret Hewitt of
Exeter represented the Catholic wing of the Church, and the
Reverend Roger Beckwith, and Dr John Fenwick represented the Evangelical wing. They were supported by
Richard Rutt, the Bishop of Leicester, and Eric Kemp, the
Bishop of Chichester, by John Gummer, chairman of the
Conservative Party, Dr Jim Packer, the Earl of Lauderdale
and others. They claimed the support of the Rev. John Stott,
but he later denied this. Groups within the Church with
deep traditional and theological differences decided to put
controversy aside for the sake of defeating the common
enemy – women. As Peter Geldard had said at the Synod in

1984, 'We may have lost a battle, but we have not lost the war.'

A letter in the *Church Times* from a Miss E.G. Blount who had 'spent thirty-five years doing a so-called man's job' said what a pity it was the that AAM did not simply wait and see what sort of job women made of being deacons. 'My experience has been that it is only when a woman is actually involved in any situation that fear and folly fly off.'

In Portsmouth, with the best of intentions but with timing that seemed a little awry, they proposed founding a 'permanent diaconate' (for men as well as women), so that it would seem proper for some people never to proceed to the priesthood.

Vivienne Faull was appointed the first woman college chaplain at Clare College at Cambridge.

A Synod working party began to discuss the form of compensation the Church would make to priests who felt obliged to leave the Church if women were ordained priest. They talked of up to ten years' salary plus a housing allowance.

In the autumn of 1985 Dr Graham Leonard, the Bishop of London, was chairman and main speaker at a private meeting at New College, Oxford, when he said that 'a split' in the Church was the likely outcome of women's ordination, a statement that was to be the beginning of an enormous controversy, with Dr Leonard's opponents perceiving it as a threat or 'blackmail', while Dr Leonard apparently believed that the schismatics were those who persisted in the idea of ordaining women.

The Church of England, he suggested, was like 'two express trains rushing towards each other on the same track'. If women were ordained he believed the Church would split irretrievably, with its more traditional members either forming an entirely new church or becoming Roman Catholics. He produced evidence from the United States claiming that there had been a 20% fall off in membership since the first women were ordained in 1974 (a figure denied by the Episcopal Church Centre in New York which claimed a loss of 20,000 members out of 2.9 million, some of these due to other issues such as the new prayerbook and racial disagreements).

A new Synod was elected and learned that some five hundred women deaconesses were waiting to become priests, this at a time when there was an annual shortfall of men offering themselves of about one hundred a year.

In Canada Dr Runcie said he was a 'gradualist' about ordaining women, fearful that their ordination might affect 'dialogue' with other churches that do not recognize the ministry of women.

Sixty-three members of Ripon College, Cuddesdon signed a statement pledging themselves to 'the furtherance of the ordination of women to the priesthood'.

The Spectator (23 November 1985) published a scornful article by Andrew Gimson on the subject of women priests with a cover showing Dr Johnson confronted by a dog on its hind legs wearing clerical robes.

In 1986 the Bishop of London started to compile a register of clergy opposed to women's ordination, advertising in the church newspapers for those who felt that the ordination of women 'would imperil the doctrinal basis of the Church of England' to get in touch with him. Over the next year he was to assemble 18,000 names.

MOW began a new magazine, *Chrysalis*, which included a 'misogynist of the Year' prize.

In the United States ECUSA, the Episcopal Church of the United States of America, gave notice that their bishops had agreed on the possibility of consecrating a woman bishop. At the same time Dr Leonard was meeting with the Foundation for Anglican Tradition Inc. who were claiming that if a woman bishop was to be elected this would be 'the final straw'.

Supportive of the Bishop was a new women's group, Women Against the Ordination of Women, set up by Margaret Hood and Margaret Hewitt. Margaret Hood felt that ordaining women was too radical an alteration in the sacramental life of the Church. She felt that the whole idea was due to 'the corrupting influence of modern feminism on the Church'.

1986 had not been a good year for the Movement for the Ordination of Women, with opposition hardening against it as its opponents became increasingly organized. But since the previous year they had been planning a huge pilgrimage to Canterbury by women and men from all over the world, in an act of thanksgiving for women's ministry. This came to be called the Joining Hands Conference, and in June 1986 they all converged on Christ Church College Canterbury, some 3000 of them. In the previous few years women around the Anglican Communion had been slowly getting to know one another and to discuss the particular obstacles they faced. A number had visited the USA either to visit Elizabeth Canham or to attend churches where they had seen women celebrate and preach. In 1984 the Moderator of MOW had been invited to Australia to help inaugurate MOW there, and she had travelled extensively in major Australian cities and had met many women. Others had made contacts at Nairobi or Sheffield, but there had been no major coming together that showed the courage and the imagination of MOW's great Canterbury pilgrimage and Conference. There were fifty women priests – from New Zealand, Canada (one of them a native American Indian), the USA, Kenya, Uganda, Brazil, Hong Kong, S. China and S. India, and other visitors, not priests, from Australia and other parts of Africa. For the first time it was possible to listen to one another's stories, to get to know one another, to exchange addresses and offer hospitality, to gain a picture of the general situation of women through the Anglican Communion. We should never be as isolated again.

The Archbishop of Canterbury received a delegation of the women at Lambeth. At Canterbury Priests for Women's Ordination held a vigil of repentance, there was a moving late night liturgy held in different parts of the Cathedral, and a huge service and Eucharist the next day at which a woman preached. There was entertainment – by the women themselves – an enormous plenary session, various smaller discussion groups and workshops, and innumerable private conversations.

The following Sunday a Canadian priest, Kate Merriman,

concelebrated with Barry Naylor, the Vicar of St Swithun's, Lewisham, and in the uproar which followed Fr Naylor said 'The Church's continuing refusal to ordain women is blatant sexual discrimination and I don't see why they should get away with it.'

The Canterbury conference produced a mixture of rage at the exclusion of women from the Church, but also a release of energy in terms of precious contacts made and promises of help exchanged between women throughout the Anglican Communion. Within two months, however, the anger was increased. At Synod, held in York in July, the major topic was the Measure to allow women ordained in other countries to celebrate the Eucharist here, the Measure known as Women Lawfully Ordained Abroad. To many women in MOW it seemed a cheap and squalid piece of legislation, deeply discriminatory against women in that it forced upon them all sorts of checks that were not incumbent upon visiting male priests – it was clear that the Measure had been deeply damaged in its long transit through Synod committees by those opposed to women priests. Nevertheless MOW supported the Measure on the grounds that it would give many people in this country a chance to experience women's ministry at the altar.

Partly because of the Bishop of London's dark warnings that if the Measure was passed it might cause 'a split', partly because of the publication of Synod's McLean Report which seemed to outline an alarming scenario of 'the complete separation of the Church of England into two bodies' (one feminist, one traditionalist) with massive resignations by clergy, partly because of a huge concerted attack by the opposition, with John Gummer literally inveighing against 'the monstrous regiment of women', the Measure gained a 60% majority, but not the two-thirds majority needed. All in all 303 Synod members had voted in favour, and 195 against. (At an earlier stage of the legislation when a simple majority was all that was required its opponents had insisted on making it 'Article 8 business', i.e. needing a bigger majority.) For good measure, a letter from the Pope deploring the ordination of women had been released by the Archbishop of Canterbury in the week before Synod (though, a little oddly, he was to speak in favour of the Measure in the Synod itself).

An article in the *Guardian* the next week caught the mood of a conversation overheard in a pub in York. 'A very Oxford voice raised to question a famous High Church conspirator "And did it really cost you 500 telephone calls to get the vote we wanted, Father?" They can be quite vicious, these Anglo-Catholics, under the smells, bells and frilly cottas.'[12]

Another piece in the *Guardian* by Walter Schwarz reported the defeat by the 'strident, well organized and well-connected anti-women minority'. It would cause, he suggested, a 'dimming' future for MOW, as they would try to push 'the tortuous legislation through against that same embattled minority'.[13]

At the same Synod the bishops, stunned by the McLean report, with its dire prognostications, decided to take the report out of the arena of discussion, asking for a six-month 'cooling off' period, before returning to a subsequent Synod with new thoughts about women's ordination. This was hailed as a significant new move. Clifford Longley, in *The Times*, quoted a bishop as saying 'The bishops seem to have stumbled upon collegiality, and they rather like it.'[14]

In August 1986, Bishop Graham Leonard announced a less than collegial move, in saying that he intended to go to Tulsa, Oklahoma in October to hold a Confirmation service for the Continuing (breakaway) Church of the Episcopal Church of the USA, and that he was 'in communion' with this Church.

On October 6, MOW held its Annual General Meeting in a private room in Church House, Westminster, and invited a woman priest, the Reverend Joyce Bennett, originally ordained in Hong Kong, but now retired and living in England, to celebrate Holy Communion there. It was both a serious act of worship, but also an expression of feeling about the vote in the July Synod. (Before the vote Dss Diana McClatchey and others had warned that the women would not be contained much longer.) The news immediately leaked out in the Press, and various kinds of hasty action were taken. The General Synod legal adviser claimed that the service was illegal (something MOW denied on the grounds that it was private). Mr Oswald Clark, Chairman of the Council of the Corporation of Church House, apologized to the Queen and the Home Secretary, apparently under the illusion that Bishop Partridge Hall was 'under the Queen's jurisdiction'. The *Guardian* asked 'What will be the substance, as opposed to the form of the regrets? Presumably that the person celebrating communion in royal precincts was of the same sex as the Queen, among the more delicate apologies to have to make.' (Actually the Hall turned out not to be under the jurisdiction of the Queen, but of Westminster Abbey.) The Archbishop of Canterbury ordered an investigation, and interviewed Bishop Peter Selby of Kingston, who had been present at the service. All hell broke loose, in fact, and, as Bishop Selby was to say, 'It is difficult to connect the quiet, natural, really rather ordinary Eucharist with all that has happened since.'

The Times wrote a rather sympathetic leader, saying that after July this was what the Church must expect. 'MOW is hardly a proscribed organization; indeed the majority of church members, and Dr Runcie himself, share its principal aim. Given that aim, it is far from astonishing that they should want an act of worship in the course of their meeting, that it should be a celebration of the Eucharist, or that they should seek an ordained woman as the celebrant.'[15] The writer all but congratulated MOW for its 'cheeky little coup'. The Archbishop, however, was reported to be 'furious'.

One woman wrote to him:

I write as a member of the Church of England for the past 61 years and as a professional social worker in a local authority social services department.

I find it almost beyond belief that, amidst all the despair and lack of faith in our society, the priority of the Church today is for an 'immediate investigation' to discover how someone ordained to do God's work in one part of the world could have had the audacity to do the same work for God in this country, and to ensure that such a thing does not happen again – at least in public.

On 31 October 1986, the House of Commons gave over-whelming support to the Measure for Deacons (Ordination of Women), voting 303–25 in favour. On the same day the Oxford Union debated the ordination of women and, in a full house, came out substantially in favour.

At Synod in November, Dr Leonard defended his visit to Tulsa, in defiance of the Archbishop's request for him not to do so, to confirm twenty-four confirmation candidates. Dss McClatchey, slightly ambiguously, defended the Eucharist at Westminster, saying that if it was illegal she apologized.

In December a public opinion poll conducted for *The Independent* newspaper by Horack and Associates showed that 68% of bishops, 60% of clergy, and 69% of laity were in favour.

In February 1987, the House of Bishops published the promised Report on women's ordination (following up the McLean Report). It came in three sections, discussing the theological issues, the principles for legislation, and the framework for the legislation including what they called 'safeguards'. While providing a better working basis for legislation than the McLean Report, it showed little grasp of the offensiveness of Church of England attitudes to women. As more than one observer pointed out, if you replaced the word 'women' with 'blacks' or even 'French-men' the document was shown immediately to be highly discriminatory. The word 'safeguard', that is the protection of parishes, clergy and bishops from the ministry of women, was used twenty-four times. Like the McLean report too, they also thought in terms of financial recompense for clergy leaving the Church over the issue of women priests. Within a week of the Report being published Dr Leonard said that in the event of women being ordained he and other bishops would make overtures to the Roman Catholic and Orthodox Churches to see if they would accept them. 'It was clear that those opposed to the ordination of women would have to make alternative arrangements.' He thought it would be impossible for those in favour of ordaining women and those against to remain within the same church. Three Conservative MPs – John Gummer, Peter Bruinvels and John Stokes – all said that they felt the same way. The Archbishop of York, John Habgood, wondered aloud why Leonard had not made these comments during the bishops' process of consultation, nor in the conclusion to which he had given formal consent. Bishop Leonard appeared to be offering to lead a breakaway. Newspapers claimed that he was seeking financial backing in the City for such a 'continuing church'.

When the Synod debate on the Bishops' Report occurred it caught to perfection the flavour of the discussion about women over the previous nine years. With both Archbishops by now declaring themselves in favour of moving, with the majority of bishops, and with many other supporters, nevertheless the sense of distaste, of doing women a favour, was profoundly shocking, as if many of the male speakers could no longer find a suitable argument to prevent the change, but their gut feelings were revealed in their lack of enthusiasm. Dr Runcie used the unfortunate analogy of the sinking of the *Titanic* (assuring the passengers that it was unlikely to happen until 1992). The opponents were much harder hitting, of course, speaking of women 'dismembering', 'destroying' the Church. Dr Leonard talked of women priests as 'a virus in the bloodstream which could never be got out' (a telling image at a moment when the full horror of AIDS was just reaching public consciousness). As a vision of misogyny the Synod was deeply frightening, although the voting was warmly in favour of accepting the Report, and of allowing the legislation to go forward. The Bishop of London issued a statement denying that he had ever said that he would lead a breakaway church or initiate schism.

Ironically, on the last day of Synod, in the evening, the first women were ordained deacon at Canterbury, an event which very nearly did not happen because of a Government mix-up in the issue of licences. Throughout the rest of the year women were ordained deacon in many parts of the country; by the end of the year there were nearly 900. In some places leading clergy stayed away from the ordinations, most notably the Bishop of Edmonton, Brian Masters. Prayer meetings were also held in protest. Earlier in February, quietly, another significant event had occurred, the initial meeting of the St Hilda Community in East London. This group of women and men, about eighteen of them to start with, had met in protest against the Synod's ruling against overseas women priests in July. All of them had been used to secretly attending celebrations by visiting women in the past. Now they decided that they would, as an act of witness, openly invite women priests visiting this country to minister to them. They would also strive for 'inclusive' language, what they called a 'non-sexist liturgy'. Thanks to the Reverend Peter Francis, himself a member of the Community, they began to meet every Sunday evening in the chapel of Queen Mary College, the University of London, in Mile End.

In March thirty-two Roman Catholics, priests, laity and religious, signed a letter warning Dr Leonard that they did not think the Roman Catholic Church should be seen as a refuge from the issue of women priests.

In April the Bishop of Sherwood, Richard Darby, said that we must not hurry in opening the priesthood to women.

At Easter the St Hilda Community held a Communion service at St Benet's, with an American woman priest, Suzanne Fageol, celebrating. Over a hundred people attended, including many clergy.

In July Ruth Wintle, a Diocesan Director of Ordinands, was made an honorary canon of Worcester Cathedral, a move that was possible because she was now, as a deacon, a 'clerk in holy orders'. Twenty members of the Federation of Catholic Priests in the Diocese of Exeter instantly objected on the grounds that Ruth Wintle had only just been made a deacon.

In August it was announced that the legislation for women priests that had been due to be brought forward to the February Synod of 1988, would be delayed until July, on the eve of the Lambeth Conference. In Australia there was a narrow defeat of the canon designed to open the priesthood to women – only four votes short of the necessary two thirds majority.

In the television programme 'In the Psychiatrist's Chair' Dr Anthony Clare interviewed the Bishop of London, and the bishop confessed his alarm at the idea of seeing a woman standing at the altar. 'My instinct when faced with her would be to take her in my arms. . . . Sexuality is built into human life and you cannot get rid of it.' He went on to expound a favourite theory that 'symbolically it is the male who takes the initiative and the female who receives' and that this meant that God was the initiator, in male style, and the priest represented him.

In response to a good deal of protest from women in this country and from overseas bishops at women's exclusion from the Lambeth 1988 Conference, it was announced in October that a day would be allowed for a full plenary presentation by women and that there would be two women priests acting as consultants, making seven women altogether. Forty-nine bishops in ECUSA agreed that they would not preside at Eucharists when in Britain while some of their priests were unable to do so.

A second woman, Muriel Pargeter, was appointed to an honorary canonry in Rochester, quickly followed by two more in Salisbury. Early in 1988 Judith Rose was made the first Rural Dean in the country in Gillingham. In February Synod debated a report about a 'permanent diaconate' – one in which members did not expect to enter the priesthood. Just after 800 women had been made deacon, many of whom *did* wish to enter the priesthood, it seemed to some speakers an odd moment to choose.

In March the World Council of Churches Ecumenical Decade for Women was launched.

On Ash Wednesday a declaration was made by the Bishop of Chichester backed by 52 bishops claiming that ordination was essentially male, and particularly warning against consecrating women bishops. At Pentecost 141 bishops, from different parts of the Anglican Communion, led by the Bishops of Bristol, Manchester and Southwark, declared their belief in the ordination of women to all three orders.

As the July Synod approached the provisions in compensation for male priests leaving the Church on account of women's ordination began to be discussed, numbers variously put at figures between 11,000 and 100. The provision was for an interest-free loan, to be paid in the first year, probably of around £16,000, payments over three years which would be the equivalent of current annual pension payments, and a £1,700 settlement grant, the whole 'golden handshake' amounting to some £30,000. Some felt that no payment should be made, one senior Church Commissioner comparing the situation to a nuclear worker who resigned on discovering that his plant was making nuclear weapons. No compensation was discussed for women deaconesses and deacons whose promotion prospects had been blighted so long by delays in legislation.

A survey of priests held by the Association for an Apostolic Ministry showed that one in ten was opposed to women's ordination. On the eve of Synod 250 opposing clergy went to Keble College, Oxford, to what was known as 'The Cost of Conscience' conference. Various legal and administrative advisers to the Church – church lawyers, diocesan registrars, and a number of archdeacons attended in order to advise clergy about the 'practicalities' of their situation if they felt unable, or at least unwilling, to continue in a church with women priests. According to reports, there was more interest in how far individuals might go in defying their bishops, than in actually leaving. 'Most of those who were there intended to stay in the Church of England and fight to the last . . .', Geoffrey Kirk was reported as saying, though there was also talk of the 'Catholic' wing taking some of the assets of the Church of England, which seemed confusing.

At the Synod Dr Runcie confused everyone by making a speech in favour of women's ordination in the first debate and then advising members to vote against it in the second, claiming that 'it is not opportune'. A handful of other bishops hitherto claiming to be supporters took the chance to vote against. The Archbishop of York made a speech in favour of the Measure, and attacking the 'headship' argument, pointing out how easily it slides into a belief about the inferiority of women. The Archdeacon of Durham suggested that some penitence was called for from men about past attitudes to women. John Gummer called upon women to sacrifice themselves. The Bishop of Birmingham also believed women should be sacrificed, in his case on the altar of ARCIC. John Sentamu, a Ugandan speaker, notably described the Church of England as a machine with the engine of a lawnmower and the brakes of a juggernaut.

Dr McLean who introduced the Draft Priests (Ordination of Women) measure said that he felt as if the Archbishop had marched us up to the top of the hill and marched us down again. The Measure was passed with all three houses getting the necessary simple majorities.

The Lambeth Conference of July 1988 was, of course, dominated by the issue of women priests (and bishops), though women were accorded no more than a half sentence in the preliminary programming, along with homosexuals and ethnic minorities, itself a piece of disingenuousness that seemed extraordinary. The problem for the Archbishop of Canterbury as *primus inter pares* in the 70-million strong Anglican Communion was how to hold the whole together when ECUSA and the Church of New Zealand were showing every intention of consecrating women bishops, some six other provinces – Canada, Uganda, Kenya, Hong Kong, South India and Brazil – already had women priests, Australia was in turmoil on the issues, and the Church of England was continuing to drag out the decision. Dr Runcie told the 525 assembled bishops that the choice was between 'independence' and 'interdependence' and he clearly hoped for the latter. An Orthodox spokesman said that ordaining women as priests would disrupt the movement towards church unity. (There were already 1,500 women ordained priest in the Anglican Communion.) Emilio Castro, general secretary of the World Council of Churches, said that there would be a 'no win' situation if churches looked at theological issues from the point of view of the reaction of others. The unity sought by churches had to be seen in context with the struggle for world liberation and world reconciliation. The Pope sent a telegram warning of the danger of 'new obstacles' (it was assumed he was referring to women priests). On the subject of women bishops, Dr Habgood thought that the answer as to whether her ordination of priests would be considered valid could be overcome if 'a male bishop should ordain with her'. In the event, the Lambeth Conference compromised on women bishops, leaving member churches to do as they thought best.

A Gallup Poll among lay Anglicans (in Britain) showed that three out of four wanted both women priests and women bishops.

In September, ECUSA did as it had said it would and elected a woman, Barbara Harris, as Suffragan Bishop of Massachusetts. Growing up in the black community of Philadelphia in the 1930s and 40s, she suffered as a child from racism, and had shown herself active in racist and sexist causes. Dr Leonard said that he would be unable to recognize her, or any confirmations or ordinations performed by her. Dr Runcie, annoyed that her election had preceded the work of a Commission on the subject of women bishops to start work in November, said, in a gloomy 'it'll end in tears' note that it would have 'far-reaching consequences'.

On 16 October, Charles Oulton published an article in the *Sunday Times* accusing the St Hilda Community of 'defying' the Church of England by holding Eucharists at St Benet's chapel, Queen Mary College, Mile End Road, at which either visiting women priests from abroad celebrated the Eucharist, or Suzanne Fageol, an American woman priest resident in this country, celebrated. The chapel was an 'ecumenical' chapel, so that Methodist women ministers were allowed to celebrate there.

Dr Leonard wrote to Suzanne Fageol saying that he requested and expected her not to celebrate any further Eucharists. The Community asked her to continue to do so, and she agreed. Eventually, after the Community had continued to celebrate for several weeks, the London Diocesan Fund, which owns St Benet's, asked their solicitors, Winckworth and Pemberton, to send a letter threatening to charge the Community with trespass. St Hilda's held one last Eucharist in the college car park to which both British and world press and television turned out in force, before taking up residence at Bow Road Church (Methodist owned), which is used by both Methodist and Anglican congregations. At the same time another woman ordained in

America, though British-born, Susan Cole-King, admitted that she held private Holy Communion services.

Preaching at a service for MOW in York Minster, Dr Habgood suggested that the St Hilda Community would impede the ordination of women.

In December the General Synod's Liturgical Commission published its report on liturgical language *Making Women Visible*.

In February 1989, Barbara Harris was consecrated bishop in Boston, with a congregation of 9000 people, many of them black. There were two objectors who were given space to speak. The Archbishop of Canterbury sent a letter to Edmond Browning, the Presiding Bishop of ECUSA, promising to pray for him. Officially, no English bishops sent Barbara Harris any good wishes, though it was said some wrote privately. Some 3000 American Roman Catholics, religious, priests and laity wrote a public letter of joy and welcome.

Meanwhile the Cost of Conscience organization had met to raise money to oppose women's ordination, and the Pope warned Dr Runcie of 'a serious deterioration' in relations if the Church of England ordained women.

In October eleven bishops – Bristol, Gloucester, Lincoln, Oxford, St Edmundsbury and Ipswich, Salisbury, Southwark, Worcester, Croydon, and Dover, led by Bishop Jim Thompson of Stepney – published a letter offering 'Catholic' support for women's ordination and distancing themselves from other Catholic opponents. 'We assert that Anglican Catholics who support the ordination of women are loyal to the tradition in which our spirituality has grown and justified in the belief that such ordinations can be a precious gift from God to enhance the catholicity of the church, and enrich her mission.' The Bishop of Edinburgh wrote an article in the *Church Times* as a Catholic Anglican strongly in favour of women priests. The Provost and chapter of Coventry declared its mind that women should be ordained to the priesthood as quickly as possible. A woman correspondent in *The Tablet* wondered aloud whether the obstacle to

Anglican/Catholic reunion was the Anglicans ordaining women, or the Roman Catholic Church *not* ordaining them.

At a Cost of Conscience meeting on the eve of the November Synod, held in Church House, attended by over a thousand priests, a good proportion of them retired, Dr Leonard took up the Archbishop's words about ordained women bringing a 'gift' to the Church. He said it was an 'unwanted' gift. He spoke of 'invasion', 'battle', 'resistance in occupied territory' and 'repelling' the invader, and recalled the threat of Napoleonic invasion. Saying that it did not want a split, the meeting, according to newspaper reports, raised £40,000 to fight against women's ordination.

On the evening before the November Synod women walked from St Martin's-in-the-Fields where they had held a service to Lambeth Palace, where they held a Eucharist and some of them stayed in all-night vigil. The following morning many of them stood outside Church House carrying the placards spelling out the word 'Waiting' as so often before.

The Measure was introduced to Synod by Canon John Dale with a quote from the mouse in *Alice in Wonderland*. 'I have been swimming about in this pool for a long time and I am very tired of it.' In his speech the Archbishop spoke, as he put it, 'from the tiller of the Church of England' and said that he recognized the danger of the yachting technique of 'going about' but that sometimes it was necessary to 'go about' to maintain direction. He talked of the need for 'courage' in legislation and Synod voted for the first clause in the Measure to ordain women priests with a 64% majority. In his speech he noted that both women and opponents of women might leave dioceses whichever way the legislation went. He said, as so often before, that he did not see women priests as an important issue 'in a world where winds of secularism blow fiercely, and the future of our world seems so precarious'. On the other hand he was aware that the Church's attitude to women seemed absurd to many outside the Church and felt that that was not 'irrelevant to evangelism'. He wished there was more consensus. David Jenkins of Durham asked the question: 'Why should good, caring and conscientious priests who are mistaken in opposing the ordination of women trouble our collective consciences more than good, caring and conscientious women who are excluded from that ministry?' Mrs Jean Mayland said that it was over twenty-two years since she had first spoken on the ordination of women. In that time her daughter had grown up, married and had a child. She did not want to wait until her grandchild was grown up before women were ordained.

Synod rejected the idea of a 'continuing' Church of those opposed to women, and it stuck to the idea of a twenty-year limit on 'safeguards'.

Provision was made for bishops and clergy who could not accept the principle of women priests. For the next twenty years they could refuse to take part in the ordination of women, or refuse to accept or work with women who had been ordained. The final outcome of the Synod was the decision to 'test the mind of the Church', that is, to send the matter out to be discussed and debated in the dioceses.

Clifford Longley, writing in *The Times*, said that moderate Anglican opinion had lost patience with 'the Anglo-Catholic party'.

> As long as the only price it demands is an attitude of tolerance, they will pay it. But once it demands that they should give up something they strongly desire, they will not. . . . Some time on Thursday afternoon the synod majority at last faced the fact that the church could not have its cake and eat it. The logic of the Bishop of London's position suddenly struck home: the moment of choice had come, and the choice was to proceed.

Rage was expressed by the opponents of women priests. William Oddie said that now they did not intend to leave, they intended to stay and become militant.

In the Salisbury diocese Stella Collins became a rural dean.

For the third time in four years the Church of Australia rejected a proposal approving the ordination of women priests.

A MORI opinion poll showed that 78% of the general public thought that the Church of England should ordain women.

In December the Rev. Dr Penelope Jamieson was elected Diocesan Bishop of Dunedin, New Zealand. She was consecrated bishop in June 1990 without incident.

The Church of Ireland agreed to ordain women, and two women were ordained. A new Synod was elected, with a number of women, for the first time in the House of Clergy. One of their earliest acts was to agree that women could be residentiary canons in Cathedrals, and that (officially) they could be rural deans.

The Bishop of Sheffield announced that he would be unable to continue as a bishop if women were ordained.

Perhaps as a New Year Resolution for 1991 William Oddie decided to become a Roman Catholic.

At the time of going to press the fate of women priests in the Church of England is still undecided. . . .

Notes

1. Sheila Fletcher, *Maude Royden: A Life* (Blackwell 1989), p. 147.
2. *Church Times*, 20 July 1916.
3. Fletcher, p. 148.
4. Fletcher, p. 140.
5. Fletcher, p. 141.
6. Brian Heeney, *The Women's Movement in the Church of England 1850–1930* (Clarendon Press 1988), p. 134.
7. Heeney.
8. Heeney.
9. This and succeeding quotations in this chapter unless otherwise attributed are drawn from material in the MOW archives.
10. C.S. Lewis, 'Priestesses in the Church?', in *God in the Dock: Essays in Theology*, ed. Walter Hooper. Collins Fount 1979.
11. Susan Dowell and Linda Hurcombe, *Dispossessed Daughters of Eve*. SCM Press 1981; 2nd ed. SPCK 1987.
12. Peter Mullen, *The Guardian*, 17 July 1986.
13. Walter Schwarz, *The Guardian*, 12 July 1986.
14. Clifford Longley, *The Times*, 21 July 1986.
15. *The Times*, 10 November 1989.

6 · Low Expectations or Natural Differences?

'Second door on the left, madam – I'm sure you'll find
something to your liking . . .'

As a Department of Education paper says 'boys are trained to be achieving, independent, competitive and self-sufficient . . . girls are trained to be comforting, dependent, co-operative and group-orientated.' Low expectations of girls while they are still young tend to lead to the acquisition of fewer qualifications and lower status jobs . . . .

300 Group publication

What is significant is that we use the term 'battered wives' rather than 'violent husbands'. It is rather as though the problem of international terrorists hijacking aeroplanes was described as 'the problem of hostages'. The effect of this renaming of the problem is to shift attention from the instigators of the violence to its victims, and the shift tends to make it easy to blame the victim for the problem and to encourage a search for solutions among the victim rather than among the violent partners.

Jan Pahl, ed, Private Violence and Public Policy Routledge & Kegan Paul 1985.

The Women's Aid Federation calculates that in any one year 12,000 women and 21,000 children will use refuge accommodation, and that at any one time about 1,000 women and 1700 children will be living in refuges. However provision of refuges is still very far from the level recommended by the Select Committee on Violence in Marriage . . . .

Select Committee Report, 1975, xxvi

We define pornography as the graphic, sexually explicit subordination of women through pictures or words, that also includes women dehumanised as sexual objects, things or commodities, enjoying pain or humiliation or rape, being tied up, cut up, mutilated, bruised or physically hurt, in postures of sexual submission or servility or display, reduced to body parts, penetrated by objects or animals, or presented in scenarios of degradation, injury, torture, shown as filthy or inferior, bleeding, bruised, or hurt in a context that makes these conditions sexual.

Catherine A. MacKinnon, 'Pornography, Civil Rights and Speech',
Frances Biddle Memorial Lecture at Harvard Law School, 5 April 1984

IN JULY 1987 Charles Green, Chairman of the Church of England's Board of Social Responsibility's Industrial and Economic Affairs Committee, introduced a report *And All that is Unseen*, subtitled *A New Look at Women and Work*. He noted the injustices to women at work described in the report. He said that 'it was right in the face of injustice that the Church should speak out, but its voice would be best heard if its own practices were just.'[1]

The Report did not attempt any very new assessment of women's working plight, but it tried to set it within a Christian context. It noted that, contrary to popular and Christian belief, women's work was not a new phenomenon. As long ago as 1850 when statistics were first kept, female employees constituted 31% of the labour force. It was sometimes implied that women ought to be at home looking after the children but, as the Report made clear, only middle-class women had ever had that option. Women's work outside the home played a crucial role in the welfare of the family – if they ceased to do external work then families below the poverty line would rise from 17% to 39%. (These figures were for 1981 – they will be higher now.) The Report also noticed that there were many families without a male income – some 900,000 single mothers and over 500,000 women with unemployed husbands. Female-headed households were the poorest, with the Finer Report of 1974 showing that low pay of women was the principal cause of poverty in one-parent families. In *Despite the Welfare State* Brown and Madge found 'conclusive evidence that women tend to be worse off than men on virtually all indices of economic status. Households headed by women are, for example, four and a half times as likely as those headed by men to be in poverty . . . . the poverty of lone mothers is particularly striking.'[2]

Moreover unemployment had hit women at least as hard as men, though a 'wangling' of the figures – the removal of married women from the unemployment figures – had made a large number of unemployed women invisible. The tragic response of many young women to unemployment was to become pregnant in order to avoid the feeling that their lives were wasted. As a result, many children were being brought up in acute poverty in some of the poorest neighbourhoods in the country.

Low pay for women stemmed from a number of causes: 1) poor expectation of girls' abilities, leading into poor education and training, and the eventual segregation of girls and women into unskilled or semi-skilled work; 2) the idea that women were destined for home and family and that this was the priority in their lives; 3) the need of some women to take time off to have their babies; 4) the fact that though many women could only cope with their family responsibilities by part-time work, part-time work tended to be low status and badly paid; 5) the belief (shown by the report to be erroneous) that women 'took jobs away from men'; 6) the inability of many women, more particularly in ethnic minorities, to work outside the home either because of their heavy burden as 'carers' – of children, old people and invalids – or because of language difficulties, and hence the ability of 'home working' organizations to exploit them. Some women working at home were earning only 50p an hour.

Within working organizations women were frequently segregated with other women, and denied access to promotion or to senior jobs. Even in professions where they predominated, such as teaching, they took a small percentage of senior positions. For example, 80% of primary school teachers are women, but 56.3% of head teachers are men. 45% of secondary teachers are women, but only 16% are heads. 57% of women work in the worst paid jobs our society has to offer – in hairdressing, catering, cleaning and other personal services. 56.9% of women work in other jobs, only 25% of them in professional jobs. At the bottom end of the scale it is clear that 'sweated labour' is as prevalent and severe as it was in Victorian times, with conditions worsening as economic times grow harder. As one woman quoted in the report put it, 'Three years ago we used to get 35.4p a blouse now you only get 15.2p. Now I work 10 or 12 hours a day – all day really from 3 in the morning to 10 at night. I have to work that long to average £70 a week.'

The Report went on to make slightly woolly suggestions about the implications of this for Church people. It did not ask as did one woman (Anita Phillips) in the Synod debate, what the implications of all this were for the employment of staff at Church House, Westminster where 'there were very few women above the level of senior executive officer' (and relatively few above secretarial level). This interesting question had been raised some years earlier (1983) in Sara Maitland's book *A Map of the New Country*.[3] 'On the question of sexism in employment the churches have allowed themselves to mirror almost exactly the patterns of the outside world.'

The issue reminded me of a well-qualified deaconess who was offered a job by the then suffragan bishop of a London diocese on condition that she gave an undertaking that if she became pregnant she would resign her job. She refused, and did not get the job. Perhaps not surprisingly she later left the Church of England and became a Methodist minister.

Part of the problem for Christians, and to a lesser extent for the rest of society, as the Report made clear, was a fixed view of women, of families, and of women's duties to husbands and children, much of it unspoken. Women *ought* to stay at home, to put husband and children before themselves and their own needs, and to put men's needs, in general and particular, before women's needs, in general and particular.

This appeared to ignore important facts; that it is economically costly for women to be underemployed and underpaid, and that their poverty affects the whole family; that society leaves nearly all the 'caring' – of young children, old people, handicapped and invalids – to women, thus making enormous savings at their expense; that 'normal' families in which the husband is the breadwinner and the wife has the choice of staying at home and looking after the children now number only about 5% of families in this country; that many women do not marry nor have children yet are still disadvantaged in employment. What seems distressingly clear is that the poverty of women is passed on to children.

There are other problems around women and work which are acutely described in Anne Borrowdale's book *A Woman's Work: Changing Christian Attitudes*.[4] It is the contention of the book that women's lives are crippled by a would-be 'Christian' attitude which depicts their lives entirely in terms of 'sacrifice'. This attitude is evident in the speeches of Mr John Gummer, among others, on the subject of women's ordination, where he suggests that it is better for women to 'suffer' an unlived vocation than to trouble the Church with their aspirations. A fellow member of Synod pointed out in a speech that when Mr Gummer calls for sacrifice, it is always someone else's sacrifice. Anne Borrowdale suggests that 'women's lives are constricted by the application of a service ethic, which demands that they serve others sacrificially, without complaint and without reward.' She does not go on to examine the secret masochistic rewards of this, the embracing of helplessness, and the abrogation of personal responsibility, but she does justly make the point that if women are to continue 'caring', then it is important both that it is freely chosen, not imposed as a 'natural' part of femininity, and that it is complemented by the development of better caring skills in men.

It was striking that both the Synod report and Anne Borrowdale's book had a ground bass of trying to persuade Christians that it was not necessarily proper to confine women to home and family, or to sacrificial roles – that for 'Christian' reasons, i.e. poverty, or women's frustration (though the hidden consequences in terms of depression, alcoholism, drugs and invalidism seem to be ignored) there should be 'concern'.

Yet the Church's report on urban priority areas, *Faith in the City*,[5] so concerned and so caring about many of the Church's failures, especially in the inner city, shows virtually no interest in the special problems of women, enquiring neither whether Christianity itself has imposed particular burdens upon them, nor whether they have special social problems regarding work, 'caring', or within the family.

The discussion in the rest of society is in a very different place, recognizing that what is at stake is male power. In the medical profession, for example, where 50% of the present intake is female, women stand only a small chance of taking the best paid jobs. Only 4% of women are surgeons, only 13% are consultants. Most get pushed to the less popular specialities – general practice, anaesthetics, psychiatry and radiology. In obstetrics and gynaecology, a popular choice with women doctors, only 11.3% hold senior posts.

Economic theory has suggested in the past that improvements in women's qualifications should have the effect of releasing women from segregated employment with all its damaging effects in terms of experience, opportunity and pay. (Women cannot claim equal pay with men unless they are working alongside men doing the same tasks as them.) Yet surveys in the 70s and early 80s suggest that there is very little change in the segregation of men and women at work except in so far as men have moved into 'women's' occupations such as nursing.

Women are substantially less well paid than men overall, the mean wage for manual employees in 1987 being £185.5 a week gross and that for women £115.3. For non-manual employees the male wage was £265.9 and for women £157.2. The overall differential meant that women were £75 a week worse off than men.

Regardless of qualification, or the type of work, women seemed to be systematically deprived of opportunity. In public bodies, for instance, there were, in 1987, 1037 women employed as against 5489 men – 67 women as against 262 men in the Department of Education and Science, 22 women as against 302 men in the Department of the Environment, 83 women as against 158 men in the DHSS, etc.

The 300 Group, started by Lesley Abdela in 1980, in recognition of her own struggles to get into Parliament, decided to investigate why fewer than 4% of the 650 MPs in this country are women, compared to some 25% in some

other European countries. They pinpointed social attitudes
to girls, and the sort of early conditioning and training they
received, as the cause of fewer qualifications and low status
jobs in many cases. They noted the poor self-confidence of
women, and saw the need to work to overcome this, to
collect and distribute information and to break down the
sort of prejudice which women so often encounter at job
interviews and in the higher as well as the lower reaches of
employment.

In June 1990 the UK Inter-Professional Group noted, in
a survey of fourteen professions, including solicitors, barris-
ters, general practitioners, surgeons, chartered accountants,
architects and engineers, that 'few had formal policies geared
to recruiting or retaining women'.[6] Solicitors, engineers and
dentists had the best record in terms of part-time work,
career breaks, child-care packages. Women are seriously
under-represented on professional bodies, and recruitment
is low for women among architects, surgeons, and engineers.

The long struggle to free women to use their gifts to the
full still goes on more than seventy years after women got
the vote. But work is far from being the only arena of
struggle, though it is one that potentially offers women
strength and independence. An even more painful, and more
hidden, area of struggle, is that concerning violence, domestic and public.

There is, significantly, a paucity of studies into domestic
violence. As Jalna Hanmer and Sheila Saunders concluded
in their study, 'the history of research funding on violence
to women in Britain to date [suggests] that social interests
are served by knowing as little as possible about this widespread social phenomenon.'[7]

In 1987 an analysis was made questioning sixty women,
contacted by letters and articles in newspapers, and maga-
zines and local radio programmes. 'Whilst not representative, the sample drew on the experience of a group of predominantly white women seldom recorded in other research:
those who do not report their experiences to welfare agencies, women from middle-class backgrounds, and women
holding professional jobs.' There was a high percentage of

sexual abuse, obscene phone calls, and sexual harassment and assault reported by the women, with 50% of the sample reporting domestic violence. This would seem to bear out the comment of the Select Committee Report on the extent of violence in family life (1975) to the effect that 'several witnesses talked to us in terms of the tip of an iceberg and this seems to be correct. Most witnesses agreed, and this is almost certainly correct, that all strata of society are involved, although the better off are perhaps less likely to seek outside help.'

A book edited by Jan Pahl in 1985, *Private Violence and Public Policy: The Needs of Battered Women and the Response of the Public Services*, commented on the significance of talking about 'battered wives' rather than 'violent husbands'.

> It is rather as though the problem of international terrorists hijacking aeroplanes was described as 'the problem of hostages'! The effect of this renaming of the problem is to shift attention from the instigators of the violence to its victims, and the shift tends to make it easy to blame the victims for the problem and to encourage a search for solutions among the victims rather than among the violent partners. This misnaming is probably no accident. A great many people hold the view that battered women are somehow responsible for what has happened to them, and this view is expressed in such statements as 'the woman must have done something to deserve it' or 'women must enjoy it really, otherwise surely they would leave'. The tragedy is that battered women themselves share the popularly held assumption that they are to blame for what is happening: they continue to blame themselves, and to feel guilty about the violence, and this is one reason why they do not leave but continue to endure the violence.[8]

Pahl says that 'there does seem to be agreement between a number of different sources which suggest that assault of wives by their husbands is by far the most common form of family violence.' The study by Dobash and Dobash[9] who analysed the police records of Edinburgh and Glasgow, bore this out, showing 776 cases of wife assault in 1974, 24.14% of all offences involving violence, and only exceeded by the 1196 assaults of male against male. Bear in mind the number of cases of wife assault *not* reported, perhaps from fear of the attacker, and it seems likely that the real figure is very much higher. Dobash suggests that only about 2% of assaults on wives and children get reported to the police.

In 1972 Erin Pizzey opened the first women's refuge, by 1978 there were some 150 groups running refuges, and now there are around 200. The Women's Aid Federation calculate that in any one year 12,000 women and 21,000 children will use refuge accommodation, and that at any one time about 1000 women and 1700 children will be living in refuges. The provision of refuges is still far from the level recommended by the Select Committee on Violence in Marriage which proposed that 'one family place per 10,000 of the population should be the initial target.'

A quite large study by Binney, Harkell and Nixon [10] indicated that 73% of women in refuges had put up with violence for three or more years; 30% of women interviewed had suffered life-threatening attacks or had been hospitalized for serious injuries such as having bones broken. 68% said that mental cruelty was one of the reasons why they left home.

Jan Pahl's study of forty-two women in refuges examined the incidents which had forced the women to leave home. 31% gave alcohol as cause or part of cause, 31% as 'personality problems', 26% as jealousy, 24% as 'expectations over performance of roles', and 24% as 'one partner going out without the other'. Sex, money and conflict over meals and mealtimes had a much lower incidence as causing trouble. But 98% reported the husband's violence towards themselves as a problem and 36% towards children.

Binney, Harkell and Nixon are interesting about sources of help for women trying to deal with or escape from domestic violence. Minister/Priest figures on the list of voluntary agencies contacted, below Samaritans (at the top of the list), Citizens' Advice Bureau and Women's Aid, but substantially above Marriage Guidance and Gingerbread. What is impressive is that 71% of women who contacted a minister or priest found the contact useful, as against 59% of Samaritans or 66% of CAB. It would be good to know more about this, whether the minister has practical resources (in terms of friendly parishioners, accommodation or funds available to him/her), or whether the help is of a less tangible kind. My own impression is that a number of church congregations, particularly in inner city areas, are alerted to the violence suffered by women, and prepared to put practical effort into helping. It is the more striking, therefore, how rigidly the Church has avoided public statements on the subject.

An even more alarming evidence of women's vulnerability to violence comes in the matter of rape, something which virtually all women fear. Ruth E. Hall's survey *Ask Any Woman: A London Enquiry into Rape and Sexual Assault*[11] showed that 81% of women were sometimes or often frightened when alone at home in the daytime, that 53% were sometimes or often frightened when out alone in the daytime, and that 76% were frightened, uneasy, or never went out at all after dark.

Most rape is not committed by strangers. Omitting 'marital rape', three out of every four rapists rape a woman known to them. Of women who have experienced rape 'once only' the majority have been assaulted by friends, boyfriends, ex-husbands, family members, neighbours, and others well known to the woman.

The term rape does not include 'indecent assault', a term which includes forced anal and oral penetration and the use of bottles and other objects; it is often more painful, humiliating and degrading, and more physically damaging, than assaults that the law recognizes as rape. Until recently the maximum penalty for indecent assault on an adult woman was two years, while it was ten for indecent assault on a man. The law has now made it the same for both sexes.

In the last year or so there has been increasing discussion of the phenomenon of rape inside marriage. This had been thought to be a rare event, but Ruth Hall's survey shows that 'it is common. In fact, for women who are or have been married, it is more common than any other rape. According to our sample, a woman who has been married is much more likely to have been raped by her husband than by any other man . . . 110 out of the 214 women who had been raped by any man had been raped by their own husbands.'

In July 1990 a case was brought against a man who had broken into his wife's parents' home in order to have sexual intercourse with his estranged wife, which he accomplished by threats. The defending barrister, Graham Buchanan, argued that according to Lord Chief Justice Hale in 1737, a husband could not be guilty of rape because his wife had given herself in the marriage contract. Mr John Milmo, prosecuting for the Crown, said that 'Hale does not represent the state of the common law in 1990' and Mr Justice Owen ruled that a husband could be guilty of rape even though the couple were not legally separated or living apart under a court order.[12]

What is gradually emerging in repeated studies is the very large number of women forced into sex by their own husbands in their own homes against their will, often as a result of threat, force or violence. Ruth Hall's study showed that home was the greatest place of fear for the women interviewed, and that married women are much more likely to have been raped by their own husbands than by any other man. Yet old beliefs about 'marital rights' made it difficult even to recognize the suffering for what it was. 'I was always told a husband can't rape his wife, which is why it took me so long to realize that that was what was happening to me. It made me feel very isolated in certain ways, such as not being able to talk about it to anyone – anyway, how can you speak about something which supposedly doesn't exist?' Out of 439 married women respondents, 22% said they had been forced into sex against their will, and of 490 common law wives the percentage was the same.

A Law Commission discussion paper, due to be published in 1991, recommends that husbands living with their wives should no longer be immune from rape charges.

Running like a thread through the abuses from which women suffer, from their poor employment record to their history of physical and sexual abuse, is the experience of powerlessness – their lack of financial resources, of political 'clout' which would get their grievances listened to more attentively, their relative lack of physical strength, though it is arguable that social conditioning has fatally encouraged women to believe that weakness is 'more sexy' than strength. In a sense it is – if what turns men on to women is power rather than love, and domination rather than a shared emotional closeness and warmth.

Pornography makes it clear that, in our society, power is perhaps the strongest of sexual turn-ons, with a huge industry organized around 'bondage'. Hard porn's business is acts of violence and humiliation against women. Soft porn's business, though it eschews whips and chains, is propagating an entirely unreal view of women as having no reality of their own that is not centred on servicing male sexual needs. Cathy Itzin, a member of the Women's Rights Committee of the National Council for Civil Liberties, who has campaigned against pornography, suggests that pornography 'functions in the same way that racist literature and speech does, to incite hatred'.[13] My own feeling is that pornographic literature is more about contempt than hatred, though the contempt appears to flow from feelings of hatred and fear. Certainly boys and adolescent men growing up in our society often reveal a frightening contempt and violence towards girls and women in their speech and attitudes, a contempt which our society secretly, or not so secretly, encourages and ratifies, offering pornography as a 'recipe book' for what sex should be like. The failure of confidence so often noted by teachers in teenage girls seems partly related to a growing awareness of the disturbing way men perceive and talk about women.

As many feminists have noted, the message about sexuality conveyed to young people is that sexual pleasure for men is initiation and dominance, and for women submission to men's wishes, in a way that is invariably depersonalizing for women. Nor is typical pornography the only way the message is conveyed. Romantic literature of the Mills and Boon or Barbara Cartland type also teaches the same lesson because it implies that the only happiness for women lies in submission to men's desires.

The suffering of women in Britain as victims of violence, sexual abuse, harassment and pornography, takes place against a world background in which women suffer much more terribly in a variety of ways: the return of *sati* as Hindu fundamentalism regains ground in India; the widespread practice of genital mutilation across a huge tract of Africa and into the Middle East (in the 1980s there were thought to be as many as 84 million women mutilated either by excision – the removal of part or all of the labia minora and the cutting of the clitoris to prevent sexual pleasure – or by infibulation – a bigger operation than the above including the stitching together of most of the vaginal opening); childhood marriages; prostitution, frequently caused by poverty but more particularly in the form of 'sex tourism' as practised by Westerners in the East; poor health; lack of literacy or of adequate formal education. These cause suffering to women all over the world. Most serious of all is the poor esteem in which women are often held – the horrible evidence of the amniocentesis tests in India which have resulted in nearly all girl foetuses being aborted reveals bottomless depths of prejudice against women, prejudice which militates strongly against women's own self-esteem.

Although Western women no longer suffer as extremely as some of their sisters, some of these forms of suffering have been known here in the not so distant past, and all of them seem to emerge from some deep, hard-to-eradicate bias against women, which may arise deep in the human unconscious, or simply be the outcome of centuries of patriarchy. Christianity, at least theoretically, believes in justice and love for all of God's creatures, yet it is oddly deaf and blind when it comes to examining and curing mistreatment of women. Their problems, as so often in human history, are obscured by the problems of others in which they are only partly included. An irony is that *Faith in the City* suggests that Church schools should be sensitive to ethnic feelings by employing members of different races as school governors. On the Committee that drew up the Report there were fifteen men and three women.

Rape, domestic violence, and the many other tragedies that afflict women more than men are played out to churches which, though individually kind, officially would rather not know. Is this because it comes closer to home than ethnic issues usually do, concerning the way many clergy treat their wives or daughters, touching upon their own deepest prejudices?

Many public statements of church leaders, either by their ignorance or their insensitivity, or occasionally by their sheer brutality, would suggest that this is the case.

Notes

1. Industrial and Economic Affairs Committee of the General Synod Board for Social Responsibility, Rosemary Dawson, ed., *And All that is Unseen*. Church House Publishing 1986.
2. Brown and Madge, *Despite the Welfare State*, A report on the SSRC/DHSS programme of research into transmitted deprivation (Heinemann 1982), p. 45; quoted in *And All that is Unseen*.
3. Sara Maitland, *A Map of the New Country* (Routledge and Kegan Paul 1983), pp. 129–32.
4. Anne Borrowdale, *A Woman's Work: Changing Christian Attitudes*. SPCK 1989.
5. Archbishop of Canterbury's Commission on Urban Priority Areas, *Faith in the City: A Call for Action by Church and Nation*. Church House Publishing 1985.
6. UK Inter-Professional Group report, quoted in the *Guardian* 28 June 1990.
7. Jalna Hanmer and Sheila Saunders, 'Blowing the Cover of the Protective Male: a Community study of Violence to Women', in Eva Gamarnikov, David H. J. Morgan, June Purvis and Daphne Taylorson, eds, *The Public and Private*. Heinemann 1983.
8. Jan Pahl, ed., *Private Violence and Public Policy: The Needs of Battered Women and the Response of the Public Services*. Routledge and Kegan Paul 1985.
9. R. E. Dobash and R. P. Dobash, *Violence against Wives: A Case Against the Patriarchy*. Shepton Mallet Open Books 1980.
10. Val Binney, Gina Harkell and Judy Nixon, eds, *Leaving Violent Men: A Study of Refuges and Housing for Battered Women*. Women's Aid Federation 1981.
11. Ruth E. Hall, *Ask any Woman: A London Enquiry into Rape and Sexual Assault*, Report of women's safety survey conducted by Women Against Rape. Falling Wall Press 1985.
12. The *Guardian*, 12 July 1990.
13. Cathy Itzin, 'Pornography Incites Hatred', *Everywoman*, No. 27 (May 19 1987), pp. 13–18.

7 · 'Of Course, There Are Far More Important...'

I would have given the Church my head, my hand, my heart. She would not have them. She did not know what to do with them. She told me to go back and do crochet in my mother's drawing-room; or if I were tired of that, to marry and look well at the head of my husband's table. You may go to the Sunday School if you like it, she said. But she gave me no training even for that. She gave me neither work to do for her, nor education for it.

Florence Nightingale in a letter to Dean Stanley, 1852 (Feminist Library)

Perhaps it is no wonder that the women were first at the Cradle and last at the Cross. They had never known a man like this Man – there never has been such another. A prophet and teacher who never nagged at them, never flattered or coaxed or patronised; who never made arch jokes about them, never treated them either as 'The Women, God help us', or 'The Ladies, God bless them!'; who rebuked without querulousness and praised without condescension; who took their questions and arguments seriously; who never mapped out their sphere for them, never urged them to be feminine or jeered at them for being female; who had no axe to grind and no uneasy male dignity to defend; who took them as he found them and was completely unselfconscious. There is no act, no sermon, no parable in the whole Gospel that borrows its pungency from female perversity; nobody could possibly guess from the words and deeds of Jesus that there was anything 'funny' about women's nature.

But we might easily deduce it from His contemporaries, and from His prophets before Him, and from His Church to this day. Women are not human; nobody shall persuade that they are human; let them say what they like, we will not believe it, though One rose from the dead.

Dorothy L. Sayers, 'The Human-not-quite-Human', in *Unpopular Opinions*. Gollancz 1946

Mary Daly on being told that Jesus was a feminist: 'Fine, wonderful. But even if he wasn't, *I am*.'

Ann Loades, ed., *Feminist Theology: a Reader*. SPCK 1990

APART FROM CONTINUALLY asserting that the time was not ripe to discuss feminism or women's ordination, church leaders and others opposed to 'giving attention' to women in the churches have returned again and again to the insulting catch phrase, 'Of course, there are far more important issues.' Synod speakers have frequently followed this up with some emotive reproof. There are people starving in Africa, war is breaking out in the Gulf, the globe is warming up at a dangerous speed, the number of churchgoers/confirmation candidates/male ordinands/Sunday-school pupils/divorced clergy/homosexuals/people living in sin is falling or rising, as the case may be, the typography of the ASB as used at the lectern to be read in church is too small (to take a recent example from the *Church Times*), and lo and behold, here we are wasting our time with something as trivial as the concerns of *women*. General Synod is not noted for the acute relevance and topicality of its discussions, but as soon as the issue of women is on the agenda it is quite sure it is wasting its time. Yet strikingly, the gallery is almost always full for such discussion (not the case with any of the other topics mentioned above), and there are always many of all persuasions burning to speak on the negligible issue.

Both the reluctance to take up the topic and the passion with which it is addressed once taken up suggest that far from being unimportant, it may be very important indeed. (And, I would want to add, perhaps more relevant to hunger in Africa, issues of sexuality, the increasing lack of public interest in the Church and many other matters than most of the ecclesiastical agenda.) The great and growing interest taken by the media in issues to do with women and the attitude of the churches, as well as by ordinary women and men in the street, would suggest that here we have a finger on a key issue, that we may be much nearer to the Church's favourite concerns of evangelism, ecumenism and social injustice than is quite convenient or welcome. Indeed, in his final (favourable) speech on the subject of women's ordination in Synod, Dr Runcie mentioned the damage the issue was doing to the Church in the eyes of outsiders.

What is most noticeable to onlookers is that women are trying very hard to say something of great importance to the Church, and *they are not being listened to*, much as Florence Nightingale was not listened to, to the disgrace and folly of the institution she sought to love and serve. Women are trying to say 'You have denied our very personhood, you have cut us out of your pictures of God, you have told us to be quiet, you have not consulted us. Now that we can speak for ourselves, we intend to do so. It is *our* church every bit as much as it is yours, and we don't like it the way it is. We don't want to be patronized or condescended to, we expect to share jobs and rites and language, theological ideas and ecclesiastical decisions, on equal terms. We dislike the "old boy network" and "jobs for the boys", and don't believe they are relevant to Christian belief. We don't want our daughters brought up on patriarchal lines or damaging theological ideas, we don't want to be flattered, or idealized, or told we are "an influence" behind the scenes. We don't want to spend all our time as secretaries, typists, flower arrangers, floor scrubbers, surplice washers, sandwich cutters, bazaar organizers, though we may choose to do our share of such things. We have strength, power, wisdom, commonsense, just as men have, and we would like to use it justly, straightforwardly and efficiently, not covertly in order to simulate weakness and helplessness.'

I wouldn't deny that there are problems in the shift of power involved, but they scarcely seem to be insoluble ones, given the new perceptivity, understanding, and some degree of goodwill.

One problem is what I would call the 'conspiracy theory' of history, an idea you sometimes hear mooted in feminist groups, that all down the centuries women have been conspired against by men. There is paranoia in this, and a willed self-pity, because although there has indeed been a terrifying oppression of women by men, it is impossible to substantiate, is indeed quite simply untrue, that men have deliberately ganged up on women to give them a hard time. Neither the Huli of Papua New Guinea (the men who were so nervous about mattresses in Chapter 2), nor the Anglo-Catholics who reveal strongly anti-feminist feelings in the Church of England (to take the two most extreme groups that spring to mind) are *primarily* concerned with hatching plots against women (though they may do so incidentally). The reasons for their actions move much more deeply within the psyche, in the form of irrational repugnance, exactly as some forms of racialism operate. Against such irrational convictions about particular groups and individuals, all advanced societies operate legal sanctions as a form of protection.

Another deep problem is that just as some men are troubled by irrational prejudices against women, so some women, it must be said, are driven by masochistic and collusive responses to male power. If it were not so, history might have been very different.

What is striking now is what a poor base this has made for happy and successful relationships between men and women – tyranny, control and 'possession' on the one hand, and subservience, obedience and 'weakness' on the other. Of course, there is a sense in which this was only the picture for public consumption. As all of us know very well, women have found their ways of obtaining power (no one can bear to live without some power) – by being possessive of their children, and sometimes continuing to dominate them into adult life, by interfering behind the scenes (like Mrs Proudie) by being capricious about, or withholding, sexual favours, by being cruel to men who loved them, by being 'taken poorly' whenever their wishes were thwarted – the power of the 'iron whim'.

Many men talk of the pain such devices have inflicted upon them, in some cases lifelong damage to their capacity to relate enjoyably to women, and this is an almost intolerable tragedy. It does not, however, justify continuing with policies which keep that kind of misery unrelieved and unchallenged. Deny women direct power, and they will obtain it covertly; it seems obvious enough. Share power with them, and very different sexual and emotional possibilities become available.

If some men feel irretrievably scarred by their encounters with their mothers or wives, I suggest that many more women feel injured by their relationships with fathers and husbands. Some are literally scarred in terrible ways – see the last chapter – some have been so wounded by different forms of abuse that they can never trust men again. And for women, unlike men, society frequently ratifies the injustices, as innumerable comments by judges, reactions by policemen, and even attitudes within the family suggest.

Just as some men in the Church would like to construct a 'separatist' Christian Church, where no women except Mary, and perhaps a few devoted female hangers-on, might intrude, so some women are drawn to separatist worship and separatist Christianity. As a temporary expedient it has uses – fears can be expressed, new ideas tentatively voiced that would be impossible in a mixed gathering.

Yet ultimately it misses the essential reality of our humanity which includes both maleness and femaleness. Whatever our wounds, whatever our fears or our sexual difficulties, it is this reality to which we all owe allegiance; to veer away from recognizing it is to move into a fantasy world, into a sort of quasi-madness. A truthful religion now must concern itself with a new relationship between women and men, new ways of thinking about that, and exploring it. And many men, as well as many women, *are* exploring it.

I remember a middle-aged German pastor listening to an argument I was having with two Anglican bishops who simply could not see what all the feminist fuss was about. 'You've got it all', they kept saying.

Finally, the German interrupted, saying to them, 'But it's *you* who haven't got it! When I suddenly saw what feminism was about – it was about three years ago now – it was a conversion! Everything was different! It was the most exciting thing that had happened to me since I became a Christian, when I was a young man.'

I do not know all that he was describing, but one thing

was very clear. He did not see 'tolerance' for feminism, a kind of lazy good-natured response to it, maybe as a favour to respected women friends, as the point. The point was something of direct salvific significance for him, of the greatest personal importance for his own growth and understanding.

Brian Wren writes about this in *What Language Shall I Borrow?* His starting point is the story of Iron Hans as retold by the American poet Robert Bly. At the bottom of a pond a hunter, who is trying to rescue his dog from drowning, discovers a 'Wild Man', covered in hair like rusty iron. The Wild Man is brought back to the hunter's castle and kept in an iron cage in the courtyard. When the hunter's small son rolls his golden ball into the cage, the Wild Man will only give it back if the child opens the cage. In order to unlock the cage, the boy has to take the key from under his mother's pillow. Then the boy and the Wild Man go to the forest together, with the boy sitting on the Man's shoulders, and they have adventures together. The Wild Man, say Wren and Bly, is male energy and exuberance, instinctive, sexual and primeval. Civilization and religion are terrified of this energy, and prefer to lock it in a cage. But when the Wild Man is let out he is not a macho brute but a gentle giant, capable of kindness and compassion. The cult of male toughness, with its warlike aggression and its physical brutality 'may be what happens when primal maleness is repressed and denied: it doesn't go away but manifests itself demonically'.

The newly freed giant might, suggests Wren, 'from his own centeredness respond to the new energy in women, facing it and valuing it because he knows his own maleness better'.

> 'Challenge and risk', says Wren to his male readers, 'are what Jesus appealed to in his male disciples when he called them to leave their nets and customs posts . . . . When we men meet the Wild Man within ourselves, and embrace him, we shall find our own wholesome, compassionate strength and be ready for new adventures. We shall be able to meet the energy and self-confidence flowering in women and partner it without domination or subservience, exchanging our gifts and

experiences . . . . We shall be able to say, in this time of women coming into their own, 'She must increase, and I must decrease.' We shall say it and not feel diminished, knowing that we are quoting a Wild Man par excellence, who gained his honoured place in history because he knew how to give place to another.

What the feminists, including Brian Wren, are suggesting, is that in the churches and out of them, we are in a new place, in which a new recognition of women, almost a *discovery* of women, is the key to our spiritual development, the development of men as well as the development of women.

One of the fears so often voiced from the time of the suffragettes onward, is that if women were given power, something sweet, desirable, beautiful about them would be lost forever. They would become imitation men, perhaps even tougher and more competitive in order to prove that they could do it. Sometimes this thought is accompanied by a good deal of sentimentality about women's intuitive, relational and connectional gifts, sentimentality of which women are often as guilty as men. It may be dangerous to separate such qualities from women's actual historical experience, their necessary adaptation to the role of bearing, protecting and cherishing new human life, and it does not make things any better to treat it as a mystical gift, a feather in women's cap, or matter for a pat on the head from Graham Leonard. A similar fear often voiced in the Church is that women, once ordained, will become totally clericalized, and instead of being a sort of counterpoint to eunuchry and clericization, a humanizing influence over against the buttoned-up black cassocks, they would join the clerical power play, and become more hierarchical than the hierarchs. I think it would be idle to deny that, in and out of the Church, some women have and will continue to do this – women are no more than human, and have their share of the human failings. Yet it is not wise, nor, ultimately, possible, to keep women in a sort of 'reserve' like rare birds since, unlike rare birds, it is evident that enormous unrealized potentialities are locked up in women that cannot come to creative fulfilment unless some risk is taken. We don't know what women would be like (nor perhaps men either) if freed from the shackles of stereotypes of what women *should* be like. Certainly one option that goes with liberation is to become greedy, power hungry, careless of the rights of others. But women, like men, need to be free to make grown up choices about their lives and how to live them. Part of the *zeitgeist* of our time has to do with discovering who women are when they are allowed grown-up status.

If the 'discovery' of women, as seems likely, is part of a discovery in the collective unconscious of humankind, then much that has been crushed, ignored, and repressed along with women would be expected to emerge. The recognition of women might lead to a different attitude to nature, to a capacity to love and cherish it, instead of dominating and abusing it; to a more sympathetic interest in the wisdoms of our 'pagan' past, not to indulge in the 'orgies' and 'goddess-worship' and fantasies about 'priestesses' which seem to titillate the opponents of women's ordination so much, but to rediscover the healing and insight and harmony with nature that was found there; to a new vision of sexuality, less concerned in making everyone conform to a Procrustes' bed of monogamous marriage than an attempt to understand the deep human longing for love and physical fulfilment and to recognize the different forms love may take.

What we are asking for is a 'new' Christianity. The 'old' Christianity was shot through with the dualism in which it claimed not to believe, with flesh fighting against spirit, reason fighting against feeling, order fighting against chaos, civilization fighting against Nature, and man fighting against woman. But perhaps we have reached the point in history where, with insight, experience and divine wisdom at last coming together, we might think in terms of integration rather than battle, armistice rather than costly war.

To suggest change, or a 'new' Christianity is, I know, instantly threatening to our nostalgia, to our dreams of an Early Christian, or medieval, or Victorian never-never Church in which these troublesome problems did not arise. It would be ludicrous not to feel gratitude for the extraordinary achievements of the Christian Church as a container for so much in art and learning and in the science of the spirit that has helped to make human beings realize their humanity. Whatever takes place now in terms of growth or change must in some sense carry that history with it, as each individual carries the blessings of parental care throughout the rest of their life. Yet something quite different is beginning to happen and it is folly to pretend that we can cram everything back out of sight and (muttering something rude about 'secular influence'), pretend that everything will go on exactly as it always did. To persist along that path is to bring about the death of the Church, an encroaching *rigor mortis* that kills our ardour and our hope.

The great Christian symbols – the angel telling Mary of the life hidden within her, the baby in its mother's arms, the man stretched upon the cross, the man who has transformed death – are symbols of equal significance to both men and women, part of the glorious sharing that we know from love-making, the movement into wholeness which must be the spiritual journey. The extraordinary expression 'making love', 'to make love', might have lent sexuality, the joining of men and women in wholeness, a very special place in Christian thought, instead of which we have scorned and denied the marvellous gift.

But now, if ever, is the moment for us to redeem the relationship between men and women, to see it as the holiest thing we have, our best possession, a window on eternity, a taste of ecstasy, the inspiration, the splendour, the statement, the root of our humanity. Or as Mozart's librettist put it in a duet between Pamina and Papageno in *The Magic Flute*:

> Ihr hoher Zweck zeigt deutlich an,
> nichts edler sei, als Weib und Mann,
> Mann und Weib, und Weib und Mann,
> reichen an die Gottheit an.

> Its lofty aim shows nothing nobler,
> nothing more noble, than woman and man,
> man and woman, and woman and man,
> striving for godliness.

This is now the spiritual path, the way to growth and to the survival of our beautiful world. There may be no other.

Bibliography

Armstrong, Karen *The Gospel According to Woman*. Hamish Hamilton 1986.

The Alternative Service Book 1980. SPCK and others.

Industrial and Economic Affairs Committee of the General Synod Board for Social Responsibility, Rosemary Dawson, ed., *And All that is Unseen: A New Look at Women and Work*. Church House Publishing 1986.

Aquinas, Thomas *Summa Theologiae: A Concise Translation*, Timothy McDermott, ed. Eyre and Spottiswood, 1989.

Baron, Dennis *Grammar and Gender*. Yale University Press 1986.

Bennett, Alan *Talking Heads*. Faber 1988.

Binney, Val, Gina Harkell, Judy Nixon, eds. *Leaving Violent Men: A Study of Refuges and Housing for Battered Women*. Women's Aid Federation 1981.

Bonaventure, St *Life of St Francis*. Everyman 1963.

Borrowdale, Anne *A Woman's Work: Changing Christian Attitudes*. SPCK 1989.

Brown, Peter *The Body and Society*. Faber 1989.

Byrne, Lavinia *Women Before God*. SPCK 1988.

Campbell, Joseph *The Power of Myth*. New York: Doubleday 1989.

Collins, Wilkie *The Woman in White*. 1860; Oxford University Press 1973.

Countryman, William L. *Dirt, Greed and Sex: Sexual Ethics in the New Testament and their Implications for Today*. SCM Press 1989.

Dinnerstein, Dorothy *The Rocking of the Cradle and the Ruling of the World*. Women's Press 1987.

Dobash, R. E. and Dobash, R. P. *Violence against Wives: A Case against the Patriarchy*. Shepton Mallet Open Books 1980.

Dowell, Susan and Linda Hurcombe *Dispossessed Daughters of Eve: Faith and Feminism*. SCM Press 1981; revised edn SPCK 1987.

Faith in the City: A Call for Action by Church and Nation. Church House Publishing 1985.

Fletcher, Sheila *Maude Royden: A Life*. Basil Blackwell 1989.

Furlong, Monica, ed. *Feminine in the Church*. SPCK 1984.

Furlong, Monica, ed. *Mirror to the Church*. SPCK 1988.

Gilligan, Carol *In a Different Voice: Psychological Theory and Women's Development*. Harvard University Press 1982.

Grey, Mary *Redeeming the Dream: Feminism, Redemption and Christian Tradition*. SPCK 1989.

Hanmer, Jalna and Mary Maynard, eds *Women, Violence and Social Control*. British Sociological Association Conference Volume, Series 23, Macmillan 1987.

Hampson, Daphne. *Theology and Feminism*. Blackwell 1990.

Hare, David. *Racing Demon*. Faber 1990.

Heeney, Brian. *The Women's Movement in the Church of England: 1850–1930*. Clarendon Press 1988.

Heine, Susanne. *Women and Early Christianity*. SCM Press 1987.

Holdsworth, Angela. *Out of the Doll's House*. BBC 1988.

King, Ursula. *Women and Spirituality: Voices of Protest and Promise*. Macmillan 1989.

Leonard, Graham, Iain MacKenzie and Peter Toon. *Let God be God*. Darton, Longman and Todd 1989.

Liturgical Commission of the General Synod of the Church of England, *Making Women Visible – Inclusive Language for Use with the Alternative Service Book*. Church House Publishing 1989.

Loades, Ann. *Searching for Lost Coins: Explorations in Christianity and Feminism*. SPCK 1987.

Loades, Ann, ed. *Feminist Theology: A Reader*. SPCK 1990.

Maitland, Sara *A Map of the New Country: Women and Christianity*. Routledge and Kegan Paul 1983.

Morley, Janet *All Desires Known*. WIT/MOW 1988.

Morley, Janet and Hannah Ward. *Celebrating Women*. WIT/MOW 1986.

Murdoch, Iris. *The Sea, the Sea*. Chatto 1978.

Oddie, William. *What Will happen to God?* SPCK 1984.

Pahl, Jan. *Private Violence and Public Policy: the needs of battered women and the response of the public services*. Routledge 1985.

Ranke-Heinemann, Uta. *Eunuchs for Heaven*. Andre Deutsch 1990.

Ruether, Rosemary Radford *Women Church*. Harper & Row 1986.

Ruether, Rosemary Radford *Sexism and God-Talk: Towards a Feminist Theology*. SCM Press 1983.

Seager, Joni and Ann Olson. *Women in the World: An International Atlas*. Pan 1986.

Spender, Dale. *Man Made Language*. Routledge and Kegan Paul 1980.

Stone, Lawrence. *The Family, Sex and Marriage in England*. Pelican 1979.

Weidman, Judith L., ed. *Christian Feminism: Visions of a New Humanity*.

Wren, Brian. *What Language Shall I Borrow? God-Talk in Worship: A Male Response to Feminist Theology*. SCM Press 1989.

Woolf, Virginia. *Three Guineas*. Hogarth Press 1938.

Index